OTHER BOOKS BY THE AUTHOR
LAUREL ELIZABETH KEYES

How To Win the Losing Fight

Seedlings From The Vine

The Inspirer

Close the Door Softly As You Go

Living Can Be Fun

I Am a Child

Angel Who Remembered

Mystery of Sex

Sundial, I Count the Sunny Hours

What's Eating You?
(Co-authored with Paul Chivington)

TONING

The Creative Power of the Voice

By

LAUREL ELIZABETH KEYES

DeVORSS & CO., *Publishers*
P.O. Box 550
Marina del Rey, CA 90294

Fourteenth Printing, 1990

Library of Congress Catalog Card Number: 73-86021
ISBN: 0-87516-176-6

Printed in the United States of America

To all those who have loved and helped me,
who have taught, guided and filled me,
as a cup
until it overflowed
with their generous giving.

Here is my offering
with the hope that it may help
to fill other cups,
other hearts and lives with joyousness.

With special appreciation to Dr. William Tiller and Ralph M. DeBit for permission to quote from their works. And, Mae Green who assisted in assembling and typing the material, and Hedda Lark whose suggestions were so helpful. Also, Elyse Coulson for her Introduction.

INTRODUCTION

In the beginning
Was the stillness
Of All That Is.
The stillness moved
And there was sound.
The sound took form
And became the word.
The word was God,
The word is God,
And then, the word was made flesh
And the individual I was given
control
Under the law of the word.

"The Voice of the Body" is vibrational activity manifesting itself upward and outward through the vehicle of the body. It is creative sound acting as movement through various levels of consciousness.

Remember when you last bent over to pick up some heavy object? What was that sound you uttered forth as you lifted up the object? A release of energy enabling you to become more charged into the movement prepared by thought. When we begin to understand and accept the vastness of this great power, then do we truly know how we each may become the director of our life pattern. Throughout Laurel's book we are ever reminded of individual responsibility. The choice is ours to make. We may be the creator or we may allow someone else to do it for us; but, whatever the decision we have each made that choice. We are indeed the thinker and can change our thoughts. And as this is so, allow the life, the joyous flow to move outward from within. This, then, is the basis by which we are healed. For as Laurel points out so well, one may easily fall into clutching an outside agent as the healing medium. Instead, enhance this aid by removing the cause through self initiative. We must learn to rely upon the natural laws which operate within and around us, for it is here

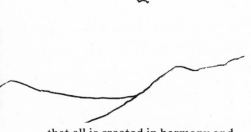

that all is created in harmony and perfection. Replace the fears, the negativity with feelings of purpose. We do have the ability to change the polarity of our field through directional application. The ability to utilize vibration as a prime mover, causing molecular structure to change. With regard to one's health this means being able to rectify and remove disharmonies through tonal vibration. Allowing the natural joy and spontaneity to flow outward from within.

Toning, indeed, offers endless possibilities; in particular, its restorative value. It is the ability of giving release and allowing the natural flow of energy to move through one's body. It acts as a stimulator, removing the obstructions so that the body may function in its proper state. Toning is much more than just a release of tension. It acts as a means by which the total expression of harmony and balance may be created and developed. It matters not whether an individual believes in it or not for toning deals directly with energy vortexes. These can be disturbed by the smallest vibration from feeling or sound, eventually to manifest as form. This, in turn, affects the electromagnetic energy of the individual. Thoughts by everyone are literally thrown into an energy force, creating either positive or negative frequencies. One can well understand that since we are living amidst a "sea of personalities" it is important and essential to clean and re-establish our field pattern each day.

There operates within the body vehicle a musical scale and when it is allowed to "sing" forth in total freedom then are we attuned to the "music of the spheres". That vibrational movement of our own creation. This form that we reside in was "made manifest" in the light of harmony, not in the sufferings of discord. So arise each day in joyous enthusiasm and know always that each word we speak or sound we make (all thought patterns) sets in motion either harmony or discord in our lives. Idle words and gossip, hostile and doubting thoughts leave their mark upon us. Let not this be the way of sound, but, instead, let it give rise to its higher aspects as the creative force it is.

ELYSE BETZ COULSON

PREFACE

A book is supposed to have a Preface, but it is my opinion that few people read prefaces. They hurry into the book to find if there is something that can be useful to them.

However, if you are one of those few who takes time to read this, let me assure you that the idea of Toning is not a theory that I am trying to prove. It is a *result* I have observed, and I have tried to report all the material in this book as factually as possible.

Toning is an ancient method of healing, which I hope will be recognized and used with new understanding now that we have more scientific explanations for it. It does not depend upon faith, nor belief in the method, any more than these are necessary to our use of electricity to provide light and energy in our daily living. There appear to be certain natural flows of energy in our bodies and if we recognize them and cooperate with them, they benefit us.

Is there a connection between Toning and glossolalia, or the speaking in tongues?

There may be an ancient tie, for glossolalia was practiced in the Eleusinian and other Mystery schools in both Western and Eastern cultures. Long before recorded history, "before the coming of churches and temples, before men were certain about the object of their worship, an inner awareness of something higher and greater than themselves filled their hearts with rapture and their tongues with praise."*

---

*Bach, Marcus, Ph.D., *The Inner Ecstasy*, Abingdon Press, Nashville, Tenn. 1969.

But as speaking in tongues is generally understood, it is a practice of Christians, dependent upon faith and considered to be a gift of the Holy Spirit.

Toning is not limited to one's religion, or lack of it. It does not require one's belief. Apparently it is not a "gift" but something available to anyone who goes through the mechanics of letting the voice express itself in a natural way. Anyone who can groan can Tone and experience its benefits.

The greatest difference is that the person who is Toning is watching the process and, after the first sigh, directs it consciously. The subjective surrender to some personality outside of one's self, acknowledged by the glossolalist, is absent. Toning is a very positive, consciously directed identification with the inner power of life, and the full awareness of the release of it at will. Rather than being submissive or losing consciousness, the Toner is extremely alert and the feeling is one of new control—of one's self, one's world and affairs; a new awareness of the unity with all life and one's inherent divinity, waiting to be recognized and claimed.

There is no mystery about Toning. It can be understood through material science, physiology and psychology as well as the most ancient concepts of man's relationship to his God.

Please try it.

CONTENTS

Chapter I

TONING—WHAT IT IS

The discovery of what we call *Toning* came about accidentally.

Most discoveries are only uncovering some ancient wisdom that has been buried in time and circumstances, but this discovery was accidental in that we did not start with a theory which we attempted to prove. Toning just happened. We watched it, and its beneficial results, then studied the influence of sound vibrations upon the body. From the result we worked back, like Newton with his apple, to the cause and the laws that brought it about.

We began with the idea that few people realize that their lives can be changed, that they have the power to control the life forces and reform their life patterns, through sound.

Consider the power we exert through ordinary speech. With words we can create images in another's mind similar to the ones held in our own.

Think, really think, what a miracle it is that a person who sees an object, such as a vase, can use sound in the form of words to cause an image of it to form in another's mind so clearly that the object could be identified among many objects. Even more, consider the miracle that enables a person to transmit a non-objective, abstract thought to another's mind. Or, stretching our small perceptions to comprehend something of the speed of light, then imagining stars, millions of light years away from our small planet. No other creatures can do that, and it is based on sound.

9

We create with words and sound. Almost all our actions and reactions result from words. It is generally accepted that we cannot think without words, or symbols, and that our thinking is limited to them. Words are tools. It is important to have a good selection at our command.

Beneath these words are the vibrations of the tone upon which they travel. Tone is the underlying force operating in our lives. To understand this, enhances our ability to create what we wish and to give form and substance to the ideas in our minds.

SOUND IS THE MEETING PLACE OF THE ABSTRACT AND MANIFESTED IDEA.

This practice of Toning began for me one day after a study group had gone and I was standing alone in the room, enjoying the stillness and the charged atmosphere which remains after such a meeting. I noticed a sensation in my chest and throat as though a force were rising, wanting to be released in sound, but it would subside again. It was the feeling that might cause one to burst into song—for no known reason—or to gasp as one might when coming upon a beautiful scene. I observed this as it rose and subsided, almost a thing apart because certainly I was doing nothing to cause this. It had a volition of its own and an apparent desire to express. It was an odd experience to both watch it and feel it, without making any effort to direct it or control it. I watched with curiosity.

I found my lips parting and my mouth opened very slightly in an easy relaxed manner so that the teeth were just barely parted. Unexpectedly a sound bubbled up, like something tossed up on a fountain spray. A single syllable emerged—"Ra."

I couldn't have been more astonished. I did not use Egyptian terms and we had not been discussing that culture. Why the sound took that form was as bewildering to me as if some other foreign language might have sprung from my throat. It came up again, paused as though frightened, but when it was not stopped it came out and soared.

To describe it I would liken it to a bird that had been caged all its life and found the door of its cage opened. It tried its wings, scarcely knowing what to expect, and finding it could be lifted in flight, it flew in delighted abandonment.

The feeling was as though these sounds came from the earth itself, and poured up through a silver tube, through my throat, effortlessly, freely as artesian water flows from the ground. I did not take a deep breath, as a singer, but the note was sustained as though supplied by a limitless source and it went into heights that I couldn't have reached normally since my voice is rather low.

I decided that I must be in some phase of meditative state so I would tape the sound and evaluate it in a more rational mood. I did. The next day, when I listened to the recording, I was still amazed. This was not "my" voice. Yet it was not someone else's as in the case of trance medium demonstrations. It belonged to my body, but I had never been able to use it in this manner before. · Perhaps that explained it. I had not used it. It had been free of my mind's domination and had expressed itself.

I concluded that since most animals have a voice—birds sing, dogs bark, cows moo, cats purr, etc.—it is our physical body that has a voice. *It is dominated by intellectual direction and it is allowed to express only as the mind dictates.*

This creative force, which does not belong to the mind, is enslaved by the mind, and is therefore rebellious. Only

11

in a groan, scream, or sigh, and in laughter, does it come out unhindered by the mind. One does not *think* a groan. It bursts through the mental restrictions and with it certain tensions are released. Many young women say that groaning during childbirth is a great help. Animals in pain groan. Pain frequently is the result of tension, and groaning is nature's way of relieving it.

Infants have a language of Toning. Their little cries and murmurings express body feelings. People remark, "The baby is singing himself to sleep." Funny little grunts and sounds that must be pleasing to him. As soon as the baby learns to combine mental images with the voice, the natural sounding is curtailed and interference is imposed upon the body-voice. This begins to close the door between the conscious and subconscious mind; between thinking and feeling communication.

As I continued to experiment with this body-voice I realized that there was much more to it than just a release of tension. Each time that I Toned, my body felt exhilarated, *alive* as it had never felt before; a feeling of wholeness and extreme wellbeing.

I became curious about the source of this energy. Knowing a woman who had properly diagnosed ulcers, tumors, and other ailments with her "x-ray vision" I asked her to watch this body-voice in expression.

She said that the Tone was a force she saw as swirling movement in the area of the reproductive organs, then appeared to draw magnetic currents up from the earth through the feet and limbs, and rose in a spiral of light to the throat area.

When I let it pass out, freely, with no attempt to control it, it appeared to cleanse the entire body, releasing tensions and congested areas. She said that the body, afterwards, had an appearance of balance, as an

12

engine that has been overhauled and all parts are working together with precision, or as a harp which has been tuned and the slack strings tightened, and the too-taut ones eased to make a harmonious whole

She noticed that when I decided to direct the Tone, the force collapsed back into the pelvic region, or into the solar plexus where it tightened into feelings I might interpret as frustration, anxiety, annoyance.

I was convinced that there had to be a relationship between this natural body-voice and the mind without conflict, and with benefit to both. Psychologists have agreed that most of our problems arise from the subconscious, the feeling nature. "When the mind and the feelings are in conflict, the feelings usually win."

Anyone who has tried to diet, stop smoking or overcome some habit knows that to think about doing it, even deciding to do it, does not assure the cooperation of the necessary willpower. This has been one of the mysteries of human functioning. Even St. Paul complained, "—for the will is present with me; but *how* to perform that which is good I find not. For the good that I would I do not; but the evil which I would not, that I do."*

Apparently the will is held by subconscious feeling, and until we can find a way to release it from that hold, to be directed by the mind, we live divided and frustrated lives.

So began the exciting search. I felt that in Toning I had been given a key to unlock this storehouse of the will.

---

*Romans 7:19-19.

Chapter II

SEARCH IN MYTH, LEGEND, RELIGIONS

Following the sound-idea as a thread back through other cultures—Grecian, Chinese, Persian, Indian, Amerindian and primitive peoples—I found that it was related to the oldest methods of healing. Two things were common in most healing rituals—sound or chanting, and rhythmic movements, either in dance or stomping.

Sound vibrations appeared to be associated with creation, whether it was of the world or our individual life patterns. "In the beginning was the Word—" Word has been translated in various ways from *Logos,* as law, archetypal pattern, etc. Philo wrote that "His image is THE WORD, a form more brilliant than fire; — the Logos is the vehicle by which God acts on the universe, and may be compared to the speech of man."* These translations indicated the importance of *vibration* rather than a word with meaning.

I began bringing these threads, from ancient philosophical teachings and religious concepts, into a pattern. I found that Chinese healers had used "singing stones" in their rituals. These were thin, flat plates of jade which, when struck, gave off musical tones. They had designated the Great Tone of Nature, *Kung,* which seems to correspond to our musical note of F. The Sufis considered *Hu to* be the creative sound. The Tibetans considered the notes of A, F sharp and G to be powerful sacred sounds. We are familiar with the importance given the words, *Aum* and *Amen.* Amen was more than a period to a

---

Morals and Dogma, by Albert Pike, 1914, p. 251.

prayer when it was first uttered. It was derived from the older "Aum" which represented all of the sounds which the human voice was capable of expressing and therefore associated with the creative principle designating God.

Pythagoras taught that sound was a creative force and that music held therapeutic benefits to the body. The Mystery Schools following these teachings associated *rhythm* with the body, *melody* with the emotions, and *harmony* lifted consciousness to spiritual awareness. This concept did not originate with Pythagoras, of course. It was used by civilizations in the remote past and he carried it on.

Along with references to sound, I found in all of the religious teachings and Mystery initiations, the traditional story of the Fall of Man. The statement that "Matter is condensed energy," attributed to Dr. Einstein, was given in older terms as "Man is condensed, or lowered, spirit." There was a definite correlation between the vibrations of spirit and the solidified form of the human body.

The word "man" coming from the Sanskrit root "manus" (thinking creature) indicated that the fall of man meant the fall of consciousness into a lower state of functioning.

One of the most common ancient beliefs, expressed in philosophies and religions, is that the soul, or individualized portion of God, was attracted to sensations and experiences to be found in the animal nature and became trapped there. It formed an identity with the animal nature and forgot its true origin and power. The Egyptians taught that the body was a prison for the soul but the latter was not condemned to eternal banishment and imprisonment. The Father of the World permits its chains to be broken, and has provided in the course of Nature the means of its escape.

All scriptural teachings are based upon the struggle of this divine part of the human to free itself from animality and return to its rightful heritage; the effort to bring the thinking and feeling qualities into accord with the harmonic pattern in which the human was created, "in the image of God."

The rational mind was considered to be an extension of the soul, or the buffer zone, between the two natures, for if the soul knowing no danger or pain had directed the physical body without recognition of the laws governing flesh and bone, it would have destroyed the vehicle.

If the animal sensations ruled the person he sank to a below-animal state, wanting only physical pleasure and satisfaction, becoming completely selfish, cruel and more vicious than an animal because he now had the ability to imagine means of satisfying the powerful urges of the animal nature. Left alone, the animal body would have crowded out all memory of the previous province of the soul's existence, lost all of the finer urges which result in expressions of love, honor, aspiration, and there would have been no art or music, fine architecture, law, science or healing—all of the achievements of man would have been denied.

With the rational mind being the interpreter for both, the ageless conflict has continued between the soul and the animal nature, or to simplify it we may say the Higher mind and the subconscious mind, for rulership of the whole. Whichever controlled the feeling process controlled the person, for the feelings are the *actors*. Unless the thoughts cause the feelings to respond, nothing is accomplished.

In the Edenic story we find this theme. Until man developed a mind capable of choosing (eating of the "fruit of the tree of knowledge of good and evil") he lived in peace. When the mind developed and began taking the consciousness into areas of sense perception, tasting, seeing, desiring, he was cut off from his effortless existence and sent out on the long journey to find his inherent divinity again through experiencing free-will and choice. These choices would bring him, eventually, either to identity with his true nature, or to suffer the "eternal" separation.

An Amerindian legend, from the Hopis, tells of creation of the First People. The Spider Woman moulded the earth, mixed with her saliva, into forms in the image of the Universal God, Sotuknang. When she uncovered them, the forms came to life. But they could not speak. Since Spider Woman received her power from Sotuknang, she had to appeal to Him to give them voice. "Also the wisdom and power to reproduce, so that they may enjoy their life and give thanks to the Creator."* Sotuknang granted this wish so the forms could speak and reproduce. (There appears to be a linking of the idea of creative productivity—the voice and sex organs. This may relate to the phenomenon of the voice change in the male at puberty.) These First People had no illness because they were of "One Heart." But when some permitted evil *feelings* to enter, they were said to have Two Hearts and then began the troubles visited upon the people.

So the legends, myths and scriptures portrayed the human state.

How could these aspects of a person, seemingly so separated, be brought back together—soul, mind and body, functioning in harmony?

---

*Book of the Hopi, Frank Waters, Viking Press, 1963.

Through "The Word!" Chants, mantras and prayers held a prominent place in achieving this union for they followed the natural pattern of creation and exercised will.

Two recurring ideas dominated the ancient teachings—the manner of creation of man (and all things), resulting from a Father-Mother union of spirit and matter, or positive and negative forces, and Will, the motivating factor by which man functioned; how he came to be and how he lived, in peace or conflict.

It became apparent that the voice is a vehicle which the mind uses for its manifestations. *It is the womb impregnated with the seed of the idea.* It is the higher creative force as the reproductive organs of the body are the lower.

It is not necessary to go into great detail in supplying references since you are not reading this book to become a scholar but to be able to use your own voice in a beneficial manner; but I would like to mention a few intimations of the Spirit-breath-sound, and matter-form relationship from varying sources.

Brahm is said to have "breathed out and creation was formed. Brahm breathed in and took the creation back into Himself."

Plato said, "The Word is number manifested by form."* We have St. John's "In the beginning was the Word." From the Hebrews there is Genesis 2:7, "And the Lord God formed man of the dust of the ground and breathed into his nostrils the breath of life; and man became a living soul." The Egyptians taught that the Father or the Spirit was the *generative* power; the

---

Morals and Dogma, Albert Pike, 1914, p. 97.

Mother, or form, was the *conceptive* power, the issue or product of this union was the Child.

In other words, everything that is results from a union of positively and negatively charged units of energy. The negative force, or mother, is that which is acted upon. In the human, it becomes the *feelings* which give form to the *idea*. But, whether the substance which takes the idea is for a statue, a garment, or is the steel and concrete giving form to a picture in the architect's mind, or is used for healing the body, the manifestation is from the surrender of negative force to positive. The negative aspect must yield and permit itself to be used, and then molds its properties into the form of the positive pattern.

There can be no harvest without seed in the soil, no child without the union of man with woman, no anything without this combination of positive and negative forces. And, it must be remembered that it is the mother which gives birth—not the father. *Feeling must be fecundated by idea or image, to bring about results.*

This may explain why many prayers, affirmations and positive thinking seem to fail. They remain bachelors. The idea has no mate to give birth to the desired offspring—mental pictures which have not stirred feelings into productivity.

Too often the mind dominates the voice ruthlessly, so it encounters resistance. It behaves as a rapist of the body forces, using them without consideration. *Feeling* then rejects the *idea*.

The feeling-voice should be wooed, lovingly, as a woman. When it is permitted its own expression, as in Toning, it feels secure and protected. It surrenders and receives the idea given it by the mind and, eager to be a part of creation, it gives birth to that form. It is joyous cooperation rather than rebellious slavery.

The conclusion which may be drawn from these old concepts is that Spirit is consciousness. It has collected around Itself a shape, or body, through which to contact experience on this more dense plane of vibration, and to raise it, transform it into Itself, through "the Word."

Chapter III

VOICE CREATES LIFE PATTERNS

Count Alfred Korzybski, father of General Semantics, referred to the cortex as a corn which had formed, over the thalamic stem, from the irritation and pressures of civilization.

In the last century we have let these pressures drive us more into our mental interests and farther away from our natural body expressions. We ride more and walk less. We sit more and stand less. We eat more and digest less. It might be said, also, that "we speak more and say less." We have grown farther away from communication with our inner nature and its needs. We cannot repress a natural creative urge without seeing evidence of the distortion.

In not too distant times people gave voice to the sounds of their body language. Men sang or whistled as they worked. Stories come to us of boatmen singing as they rowed, railroad workers pounding rails to ties with accompanying rhythms or song. Mothers hummed as they worked—usually nameless little songs that reflected their emotions; songs stirring with the whir of a spinning wheel, the thumping of a churn-dasher, or the hum of a sewing machine. Since woman first cradled her baby in her arms she has let her heart express in tender murmurings, to heal a hurt or dispel a fear.

Folk songs and Negro spirituals were born in this way. Even at the beginning of this century it was a common thing for family and friends to gather around the piano in the evening and sing. While these songs were patterned, they afforded opportunity for each person to express himself. They sang softly or loudly, took pride in their singing or made an effort to improve it, but in this outlet there was a therapeutic process taking place, one which is sadly lacking now in the person who sits in a chair silently watching a TV program or having to listen to a professional sing from some platform. Many people went to church more for the opportunity to sing out loudly in the sociability it afforded than for the sermon. Now there are choirs paid to sing, and while it may sound better to the listener, each body denied the joyful soaring of its own voice is suffering.

This may be one of the clues to the increase in neurosis and psychosomatic illness. Certainly there is growing evidence that noise and discordant sound (as in some of the so-called music) supplanting the natural voice expressions is in part to blame.

Dorothy Retallack did an interesting study on the effect of sound on plant life. She had been intrigued by the reference to this in the first edition of this book and did the experiments at Colorado Womans' College in Denver.*

In one of the most revealing of these experiments, the plants were subjected to a radio station which broadcast rock, and another which programmed classical and religious music. The plants leaned away from the rock broadcasting, some at 80° angles. Their root structures were shallow and these, too, grew away from the sound. Petunias refused to bloom. In contrast, squash vines wrapped themselves around the radio playing harmonious and religious music and there were six lovely blossoms on the

---

*Sound of Music and Plants, by Dorothy Retallack, DeVorss & Co., 1973.

petunia plant. Roots of these plants were plentiful and strong, the plants luxuriant in growth.

Her further studies on the response of plant life to sound caused her to comment, "I just can't help thinking that there is some combination of harmonic sounds that would improve human growth and heal illness."

Seeing plants react in this manner to sound causes us to wonder how much irreparable damage is being done to the human structure with civilization's increasing noise levels. It would seem that of all the pollutions about which we show concern, sound pollution could be the most dangerous. Yet it is something each of us can help to control, in our own lives, by the manner in which we use our voices.

By releasing tensions and stimulating circulation and nerve energy in the body, Toning is a natural method of healing. It releases the pattern of perfection within each person. Wonderful as are healing helps such as medicine, surgery, etc., they are limited by the patient's ability to accept them. Unless there is full cooperation with the subconscious mind, the desired healing will not be lasting.

Physicians often are baffled when a patient has been cured of ulcers or some ailment and returns later with tumors, migraines or some other disorder. The patient's body was not in harmony with the pattern in his field. Surgery or medicine cannot eliminate hatred, fear or other feelings which cause deep-rooted problems. Seldom can talking about them (using the mind's concepts and symbols) result in changing the feelings; yet joyous feeling is so necessary for permanent correction.

Dr. William Tiller, who is with the Department of Materials Science at Stanford University and a Guggenheim Fellowship member among other titles and honors, brings new light to this old problem when he states, "All

23

illness has its origin in a disharmony between the mind and spirit levels of the entity and that of the universal pattern for the entity.—Thus, healing at the physical or even the etheric level is only temporary if the basic pattern at the mind and spirit level remains unchanged."*

Most of us have watched cobwebs form when dust particles collect in a pattern made by air currents from a furnace or window, and while this is not an esthetic referent, it seems to me that as Tone goes out, it collects substance from the world around, forming a very tangible manifestation.

When fine sand or sugar is sprinkled on a drumhead and put in contact with the vibrations coming from a violin or piano, the granules take on various geometric patterns; so again we have evidence that sound can move matter; vibrations can cause changes in the molecular structures.

The tone of a person's voice is highly indicative of his state, not only of health but of affairs. If the person's voice is whiny and has a sucking in or gasping sound, the person has a negative health condition and is often so discouraged or hopeless that self-pity becomes the positive polarity (instead of health), and no healing can be effected until the person reverses his tonal pattern. He is like a bottomless pit that will absorb all the help and attention given him, but will not use it to help himself. He seems to cling to the problem or illness since it is what gains attention and importance for himself! His affairs are as sick as he is. He draws in negative conditions as a magnet attracts iron.

---

*"Radionics, Radiesthesia & Physics," *Varieties of Healing Experience*. Dr. William Tiller, Academy of Parapsychology & Medicine, Los Altos, Ca., 1971.

One can almost see the force of the voice of such a person spiraling counter-clockwise and down, rather than clockwise and up, which is a condition of health.

Then there is the tone which is thrust out but covers hostility, resentment and other negative conditions so that the person is always in trouble, in conflict, "fighting for everything" he has and generally is disliked and unhappy. This type of person never asks a question—he demands an answer; and seldom gets a satisfactory one because he frightens the person asked and causes so much confusion and chaos that inefficiency flourishes wherever he is. Unfortunately this type of person is often in a position of authority (by his forcefulness) and just by the tone of his voice breeds hate and rebellion around himself. He is accident-prone and trouble-saturated. In illness he is the one who has heart attacks, strokes, broken bones, falls and violent accidents; by his tone he attracts to him what he is—violence.

Conversely, the sucking-in, whining tone attracts lingering illness: cancer, asthma, allergies, tumors, rheumatism, arthritis, etc.

By the manner in which we speak, every hour of our lives, we set the pattern for our lives. When we realize the vastness of this power, we can appreciate the admonition in the Bible that we shall be held accountable for our every word. At least, the tone in which it is spoken!

Frequently I have watched amazing results come about in illness by just causing the person to change his tone in speaking. Instead of a sucking-in tone, to *thrust* his words out with vigor. By using his own voice to do this, he seems to change the polarity of his "field" and a healthy condition results.

One notable example was a woman who was suffering from mononucleosis and had been sent home, in her own

25

conviction, "to die." She was in bed, of course, and so weak that it was difficult for her to speak over the telephone. I explained the Toning idea to her and asked her to work with me repeating simple words such as "I am going to get out of bed and do things that I want to do," but in a thrusting, positive way. (Even the word "thrust" causes vigor. The *th* sound is one of positive push. One could hardly draw in his last dying breath with a good 'th' sound.)

"Give it more THRUST," I encouraged her, and finally, with some indignation, she responded, "I am thrusting my words out." From that moment it seemed the force was reversed from negative to positive polarity. The next day she was not only out of bed, but was doing some housework, and on the third day she drove to a nearby town to hear a lecture. There was no return of the illness. That day of changing her voice pattern began the change of her health.

It is not enough to let the negative feelings be released and expressed. Feelings of purpose must replace them— the person must be inspired to feel that he is noble, good and worthy because that is his true state—the pattern of perfection in his field.

"What gets your attention gets you." When one dwells upon his weaknesses and faults he pours more energy into them and they seem to grow. He talks about them, giving new birth to them so that in turn he has more troubles to talk about. It becomes a vicious circle.

Some people insist that they would be hypocrites to say they feel good or happy when they feel inferior and miserable. They want to be "themselves." But, what self? Why identify with one's lowest nature? Why not identify with the inherent perfect pattern in the field as Dr. Tiller described it? That is the real Self.

26

"Be ye perfect, even as your father in heaven is perfect" is not a pretty but impossible dream. It is a direction, a statement of fact. We are fashioned "in the image of God" (perfection). Until we reinstate ourselves in it, become one with that pattern, sorrows and problems are the natural results of separation.

When illness or misfortune comes into a life, a person often cries, "Why should this happen to me? Why does God punish me so?"

To ask that is about as sensible as to step off a 10-story building and, finding one's self crushed on the ground, ask, "Why does the ground punish me so?"

We should ask, "What have I done to separate me from my right pattern of health? What lesson am I to learn from this?" If electrical current does not flow into an appliance it is not that it is trying to punish it—it is probable that a fuse has been blown by overuse, or the appliance has broken down from neglect. Let us find the cause and correct it. Refuse to suffer for nothing! Learn from it and get your value's worth from the payment.

We do not live in a world common to all people. We live in our private little cocoon worlds which we create from our thoughts and feelings—our memories, desires, reactions and evaluations. *These are the substances which form upon the forces of life,* as cobwebs form upon currents of air, according to our conscious or unconscious direction. "We make our habitation, as the worm spins silk, and dwell therein."

As an analogy, picture a man taking a puppy on a leash for a walk. For the puppy's protection the leash is held in the master's hand. Without it the puppy might dash out in front of a car, fall into some other danger, or be lost. If the puppy decides to rush headlong after a cat, he comes to the end of the leash and crashes to a

27

painful halt. He gets up, looks at his master and must wonder, "How can he hurt me so if he loves me?"

When the dog learns obedience to the master's commands, the leash is removed. It is no longer necessary for the dog's safety.

When we dash off on our own desires, too often unwisely, we come to "the end of our rope," and are jerked up. The severity of the upsetting tumble depends upon the speed we are going in our independent pursuit. It is not the Master's wish to hurt us, but to save us from complete destruction the rope is placed around us.

Through Toning the body has opportunity to slip into, and rest in our perfect pattern. It surrenders to the highest which the soul can direct the mind to imagine. In this the person finds peace and the answers to problems. His heritage of joy and wellbeing is claimed.

Chapter IV

HOW TO TONE

One of the aids to healing which Toning provides is cleansing of the field. Another is to invite the subconscious mind to cooperate with ideas held in the rational mind and to bring about a condition of wholeness—body, mind and soul, for the person.

Stand erect, with feet several inches apart. Stretch both arms high and let them drop back, shoulders swinging on the spine as a cross bar rests on top of a T, in perfect balance.

The eyes must be closed. Begin to look inward, and *feel*.

Let the torso ride on the pelvic boney structure with the feeling that the hip bones protrude a little as headlights on an automobile. (This is to counteract our usual tendency to cave in and bend forward.) Standing erect should cause no strain but give an easy, relaxed feeling. Let the body sway as a flower on its stalk in a breeze.

It is natural for all living things to move. The tides move, sap rises and falls in trees, plants move. It is unnatural for the body to be held in a rigid position. Let it sway slightly to get the feeling of the pulsation of life within it; the heartbeat, the flow of blood, the rhythm of breathing—finally, the oneness with all life throbbing in all of nature.

Feeling this magical process of aliveness within and around you, *let your body speak*. Relax the jaws so that the teeth are slightly parted. Let sound come up from it, not down upon it from the mind, but up from your feet. Let the body groan. It may be only an audible deep

29

sigh but it is a feeling of release, of emptying out, of resting. Encourage it to be vocal. Always start with low groans.

Let the body groan as long as it likes and with abandon. You may think that you have nothing to groan about, but you will be surprised. All the hurts, physical and emotional, which you have received are buried in your subconscious memory, and groaning offers a release for them. Once the door is opened, repressed feelings of your entire life may begin to flow out. The groan may burst into protests such as "I'm tired of everything, my work, my family, of living, of struggling. I want freedom." Or, the voice may soar off into bird-like singing or spontaneous outpourings of worship or prayer. (For these reasons, Toning should be practiced alone whenever possible. At least the first few times.)

Whatever happens, do not let the mind influence it. Make the mind obedient, be still. Let it observe as it would a stage play where it would not presume to get into the act. Watch. And, learn something of the host of this body house in which you, as consciousness, are only a guest.

Even in the first Toning session you will find that the voice, after groaning, is inclined to rise, siren-like, drop back and rise again, over and over until it reaches higher notes without effort.

The session may last ten minutes or an hour, but when the body feels cleansed *a sigh is released* and you know that the body-voice is satisfied. The involuntary sigh is the signal. You feel good. As though something had been accomplished, and you had brought yourself together into a harmonious whole. Confidence permeates you.

As you read this, notice how many times the word "let" is used. This is the most important factor of Toning. Let the body be free, let the voice be free, let health emerge. Don't strive, or impose direction upon the voice. You are going to learn to unfold from the inside out.

Toning stimulates the energy flowing in the body, causing a healthy glow. Even the medical phrase "body tone" indicates unconscious awareness of this. (How often we speak better than we know.) It releases the "Imprisoned Splendor" by bringing the mind and body together so that the inherent perfection of the field can manifest in both cell structure and ideal without interference or tensions.

As soon as the sigh is released and cleansing for that time is complete, something must be offered to fill the emptied cup. If possible sit down for a few moments and enjoy the sense of peace which comes, read from a favorite book of inspiration. Let yourself enjoy the feeling of new aliveness, inside. You may wish to follow Toning with a meditation period, or sing a happy song. Whatever you do afterwards, you will be aware that you have "fastened the light" in yourself for the day.

You may object that there is no time for this. Is there time to be ill? Time to be unhappy, rushed, scattered? There is always time if we wish to do a thing.

For the busy, harassed mother, great benefits will be noticed if she will arise a half hour before the family in the morning, go into another room and Tone softly. It is a delightful feeling that one enjoys—a feeling of being ahead, instead of being rushed to keep up—to feel perfectly in control of one's self and the day and whatever it may bring. Tell your subconscious mind that "some lovely thing is going to happen today," and it will begin to look for it, and bring it about.

Toning should be done upon first awaking or in the shower. Later in the day is better than not at all, but

31

early morning helps you "pull yourself together" and set the pattern for the day.

While each individual's Toning pattern is different, as is his thumb print, you may feel that you have really found it when it follows this general pattern.

First phase: Relaxing the body in standing position, if possible. It can be done sitting in a car or in a chair, or even while lying in bed if one is ill, but let the body express itself in sound. Groan and watch the sound rise. The feeling is that an offering is being made. The life force within is eager to rise and be free.

Second phase: After the first few very low groans it will rise. Do not force it. Let it go where it wishes, until it rises to what it feels is a smooth high and flawless note. (Any strain defeats the purpose. Toning is release. Strain is imposed by the mind.)

It may be a new experience for you to feel an effortless action taking place in your body, yet this is the secret of good health, good emotional balance and clear thinking—to flow with life instead of fighting it.

Notice how your voice seems to long to rise into freedom. Let your mind witness this feeling and *expect your voice to rise* with the sense of joyous release that a child feels in throwing a ball to the sky.

Finally the body will be satisfied with what it feels is a perfect tone. This is the jewel which it offers in reverence to life. There will be a deep, contented sigh following that note. It is the signal that there is peace in your nature and your subconscious mind is ready to serve you. This ends the cleansing stage. Enjoy the feeling of being put together, as though you were wrapped in an impenetrable armour and filled with love for the whole world.

Now you are ready to accomplish something—to create

with your voice, to Tone for others or some desired condition in your own life.

One may use the notes, A, B, C, etc., as described in more detail later on. The vowel sounds can be used as vessels into which the Tone is poured and carried upwards. A-O-U-eeeeee.

Beginning with the "Ah" sound, watch the natural progression. Watch the tongue and mouth in the formation of the sounds.

"Ah" lets the tongue lie in a relaxed manner. Oh," begins to draw the lip muscles into form and tightens control on the tongue. The "U" or oo-sound, as in *muse,* further controls the lips and raises the tongue. In the "E" sound, the tongue and breath are raised and all of the sound seems lifted from the throat to the head and there is a union of forces there.

"E" sound is very powerful, especially if one consciously causes it to resonate in the upper part of the head. It should not be done too strenuously or long in the beginning. Find your own comfortable way, your own rhythm, through experience. Tone until you feel good, newly alive, enthusiastic.

It should cause one to feel that one is pilot of one's own craft, in complete command, flying above any difficulties and using even adverse winds to carry one to the desired destination.

Once you have found the benefit of Toning you will not give it up or let anything prevent your doing it. You will look back on your pre-Toning days as being only half alive, half a person. As one woman said, "I may forget to put my shoes on, or eat breakfast or a lot of things, but I wouldn't think of trying to face my day without Toning."

One may have felt depressed, ill, exhausted—it doesn't

matter. From the first sound of Toning one notices a difference—it is taking *control* of one's body and life and, regardless of the negative condition, within a few minutes an improvement will be noticed. Toning shatters the negative condition. It is plugging into a power station and being recharged. It is using your will power.

It is the voice which releases the power in the body—starts the motor running so the driver (the mind) may direct the car to where he wishes to go.

Your day isn't alive until you have begun its creation with "the Word."

It has been suggested that if one Toned, resonating the sound in a particular part of the brain which controlled an affected area of the body, correction might be made through that means. (This would amount to a sonar-acupuncture in the brain?) It sounds reasonable. Yogins have controlled their bodies for centuries with their science of brain and breath control. We know that a touch of a probe upon the brain will cause certain parts of the body to twitch, certain memories to be recalled and re-lived vividly. There is so much yet to be learned about the brain. Here might be an exciting frontier to explore, through sound.

When one has a pain somewhere in the body one begins Toning as low as the voice can reach, and slowly raises the pitch, as a siren sound rises. One will find that *there is a Tone which resonates with the pain and relieves the tension.* This is all done with sensitivity to feeling. To get an idea of this, place your finger against your nose and hum, directing the sound to that spot. Notice the sensation, inside, of the resonance. While this is not as definite in other parts of the body, it can be determined, and that is the tone that will relieve pain. Every pain has its companion Tone and by pulsating the Tone softly for a time—as long as it feels good, 15 minutes or an hour —the pain will be relieved or eliminated. It is an escape valve for the pain because it is breaking up the tension which we label "pain" and it brings new life energy to that place. It is an inner sonar massage.

Many times, in a public lecture, I have asked someone in the audience, who has a pain, to come up and let this technique be demonstrated. As I stand facing the person, eyes closed and concentrating on the feeling of the sound, I start Toning very low and slowly, letting the sound scan the body. When the sound returns to me from the afflicted area I know it. It is an indescribable sensation—sticky—thick—there is no proper word but it is noticeable to me. I ask the person if that sound would seem more comfortable a little higher or lower—"This is the feeling that you have an inner itch and I am trying to let the sound scratch it—lower or higher?" This helps the person concentrate upon the exact area of distress. Then I pulsate the sound in a rhythmic manner, until my body sighs. Then I reach a high note with the feeling of energizing their own source of energy and let the sound sweep down through the body, perhaps 2 or 3 times.

The delightful thing is to witness their surprise when I open my eyes. "It's gone!" they exclaim in total unbelief. But it is gone, or at least helped. And I assure them that this is what they can do for themselves.

The problem may not always lie in the area of the pain. One interesting demonstration was that of a man who volunteered to have his headache relieved. He had been suffering with increasing and intensifying headaches. I started Toning at his feet and as the sound moved up I traced it up the inside of his leg, around the hip to his back, up the back to his neck, and finally to his head.

But I could not hold the sound in his head area because it couldn't get past the "sticky" place in his foot.

"I'm sorry," I told him. "But the trouble seems to lie in your left foot."

"Nothing is wrong with my feet." He insisted.

The Tone wouldn't move up.

"Would you please sit down and press the inside of your arch? This is something which is puzzling me very much."

He sat down. He was wearing flat, hard-soled barefoot-sandals. He began probing the area of the arch and he let out a yell, "Wow—that IS sore. I didn't know."

He was a heavy man and wearing that type of sandal gave no support to his arch.

"Maybe I should start wearing shoes," he decided.

Having found the source of the pain, we worked with sound all the way up and he found that the headache was eased and in a short time was gone.

When I demonstrate this technique it is in no manner intended that I am a "healer." Only to convince people that the sound *they* produce with their own voices can have an effect upon their bodies.

The Tone does not have to be prolonged or noticeable to people around. One woman told me that she had a heart condition which caused "catches of pain" and she seemed unable to breathe until she could reach her medication, which often was awkward. "By Toning softly I find relief almost at once. Even if I am riding in a car or bus, or in a room where there is a radio or conversation going on, no one else would be aware of it. If they heard they might just think I was humming a little."

This type of Toning is more of an audible deep sigh than verbal. It is always done with the exhaling breath

—release—release—release. Toning assists *healing from the inside out.*

Most methods of healing begin on the outside and attempt to reach the trouble. Sometimes the surface is healed but the cause is not removed. Toning releases the health which is natural to the body but which is denied expression by obstructions of the natural flow of energy in the body. This does not deny other means of healing. It just assists the healing process because it is cleansing, harmonious and stimulating to healthy cell growth.

The question arises, "Why doesn't Toning stimulate all cell growth, such as cancer cells?"

Referring to Dr. Tiller's statement about the field, Toning stimulates only that which is natural to the body's field-pattern. We may see it in this way; in a neglected or unoccupied house, dirt, rubbish and mold may accumulate, but when the owner cleans it he throws out only the foreign materials, not the furniture and things which belong to him. He restores it to its proper state.

Toning does this for the body. It cleans the body house of its rubbish and puts it back in right order.

It is well known that a cell will continue to reproduce itself almost endlessly, given proper nutrients, if it is separated from its natural environment in the body. Cancer cells are those cells which for some reason have become independent of the field-pattern of the body, we are told. They have "withdrawn and are doing their own thing," with complete disregard for their relationship to the whole organism. When this action is observed anywhere in nature we find destruction—in physics, a body, man's disregard for his environment which results in destruction of natural resources, in society, religion or education. It is becoming more and more evident that

37

any form, a body or structured concept, in order to exist in a healthy, useful manner must follow the Logos; the perfect pattern of the whole. This does not mean that there are no new ways to be found which may lead to improvement but they must be *within the Pattern of Creation* which is based on balance and harmony, if they are to last, and be beneficial as intended.

This is the reason the older cultures, whose evidences we see in the remarkable dimensions of the Pyramid of Giza, Stonehenge, etc., adhered to mathematical and astronomical calculations. (The latest estimate of the pyramid's building as given by C. 14, is 71,000 B.C.*) Such structures endured because they were built within the pattern of natural laws.

Every word that we speak, or sound that we make, sets in motion either harmony or discord in our lives. Again, that verse which says, "Not that which goeth into the mouth defileth a man; but that which cometh out of the mouth, this defileth a man," can have new meaning. Idle words, sharp sarcastic words, hostile and fearful words leave their mark upon us. That is why we should avail ourselves of a daily Tone bath.

---

*The Pyramid and its Relationship to Biocosmic Energy, G. Patrick Flanagan, Ph.D., Glendale, Calif. 1972.

Chapter V

THE NEED FOR DAILY TONING

The need for daily Toning may be better understood when we have a clearer picture of how the vibrations of thought, emotions and voice relate to the body and why they have such a strong influence upon us.

As you probably know, we have a colloidal system, along with all the other wonderful mechanisms of our being. The word *colloid* comes from the Greek, meaning *glue*. It constitutes the connecting link between the psychic nature and the physiological organism.

From atom to molecule to colloid, we are dealing with energy vortexes. A small speck seen under a microscope is a thousand times larger than a colloid—which, like the atom, is not a "thing" but a unit of energy. Yet, each of these is a tiny universe with the same functioning as a solar system. (These assertions are made through the ability of science to register the wave lengths and frequencies and measure them mathematically.)

If we take the sphere of a substance, a drop of water for instance, and make two spheres of the substance, the volume of the two will be equal to the one but the surface dimensions of the two smaller spheres will be greater than the surface of the larger one. The smaller the units, the greater becomes the surface area.

The surface of vast numbers of colloids contained in a sphere the size of a #10 buckshot is estimated to equal about one-half acre. Or, to give a picture of this to your subconscious mind to grasp, if you took your fingernails and rolled them into little balls, there would be enough colloidal surface contained in them to spread over a city block.

How many such little balls do you think your body contains? This will give you some idea of the immense area contained within you; probably thousands of acres of quivering, sensitive "glue" which holds you together, but which can be disturbed by the smallest vibration from feeling or sound!

And while colloids are an energy system, when conditions cause them to "condense" they pass into a crystalloid state that becomes form. That is why emotions and sound disturbing the colloidal level eventually manifest in the physical body.

Every thought that you and everyone else thinks has its force in energy. Every feeling that you and others have is thrown into the energy frequencies. We exist in an ocean of positive and negative forces and we could easily drown if it were not for the protection we have in establishing control of our colloidal system through the proper voice tones. These form and concentrate the patterns of our fields. And, if I understand Dr. Tiller's theory correctly, the colloidal energy is the "substance" of the field.

It is evident from this that no one can afford to indulge in emotional storms, anger, fear, self-pity and such negative influences, or identify with or react to them when expressed by others; and why it is essential that we clean and re-establish our field pattern every day and tune it to positive polarity.

"Thought-feeling forces have profound influence in terms of electromagnetic energy upon the surface tensions of the colloids. When one permits inharmonious frequencies to register on the colloidal surface, it goes negative. Other positive forces will register on the negative and will affect the structure of the protoplasmic phase in the configurating process and will ultimately become crystalloid — that is, organic entities which we label tumors, cancer, and other illness. That is the end product of what begins in the colloidal world.

"It is so important that the surface of the colloidal field be positively charged. And it is very simple: *maintain enthusiasm*. When you pour love and interest into whatever you are doing, you are automatically insulating this field against inharmonious conditions. Internal harmony is an insulator against external inharmony."*

Toning, chanting, verbal prayer, all of these direct the voice in calmness and confidence, giving the needed positive charge to the miles of "glue" surface. It impresses ripples of enthusiasm and joy upon the field, in morning Toning, and makes it an invisible armor for your day.

Each day in the cloisters of our individual lives, we can use a breath and sound method to cleanse our bodies and fields. This applies to problems as well as healing.

After the initial morning Toning, sit comfortably with your back straight, head erect. Close your eyes and inwardly watch your breath slow to about 4 times a minute.

Visualize a pure white light, such as sunlight on snow, pouring in through the top of your head. Feel it go down the spine and out through the nerves to every part of your body. Inhale this light. Think of yourself as attached to "The Father" by this cord of Light. Through its pulsations, as you breathe, you are formed, sustained and give birth to consciousness of your divine nature. Through your mother you were born on the physical level. Through this

---

Colloidal Structure, by Ralph M. DeBit. Rowny Press, Santa Barbara, Ca., 1957.

divine Father you are born on the level of consciousness.

You become aware of your rightful heritage; that you need not be a slave to the circumstances (which you have created through ignorance) but can be a master of the world you create with your ideas, feelings and voice.

With each breath that you inhale feel this light flooding through you from above, down your spine, out through the nerves to every portion of your body. *Feel,* "with every breath I inhale I am renewed and restored in the perfection in which I was created." Feel your body fill with light.

With each breath that you exhale, visualize this changed to a cool, violet cleansing light flowing up through and around you, dissolving all of the shadows and problems in your life. Make a soft humming sound and feel, "with every breath that I exhale, I release all imperfections and the memory of every unpleasant experience, and I am left cleansed, healed and filled with peace."

Practice this for as long as convenient. It should be at least 10 minutes.

For the need of the subconscious to see pictures, visualize a cup of black ink in which you let clear water drop a drop at a time. Let it dilute and replace the ink until you eventually have the cup filled with clean water. Each breath can help cleanse your body of impurities. This is not just an idea of the mind. You are *feeling* the breath enter your nostrils and go into your body so the subconscious realizes that *something is happening.* Therefore it may expect a result—change. It has entered into the process and some of its will is being released to your guidance.

Now draw a deep breath, keeping the visualization of the scintillating, healing power of the light going down the spine and out through the nerves, and direct it to any affected or painful area.

Hold your breath there, feeling that you are forcing life to heal there. Feel the throb as you concentrate on that area. Then, exhale suddenly with a groan and feel the breath force out any imperfection from those cells, and that they are freed for their normal expression or healthy growth. Feel the light increase in that place as you visualize the "divine fire" in the nucleus of the cells devour any germ or intruder. (This is called bonfiring. The more trash heaped upon a bonfire, the brighter the blaze.)

One of the ways to feel control of pain, at least to have periods of freedom from it, is to use this breath and sound method. Draw in the breath and force it to the area of pain and feel the breath *push out,* or flush out the pain. It seems to leave as long as the breath is held, and then released in this manner.

With each exhalation, the intensity of the pain appears to diminish, for the subconscious mind has accepted the picture of the diluted ink in the cup and *expects* less pain to remain after each breath is released. It is being washed away.

A person, dying with terminal cancer, told me that "the greatest pain was the fear that I had no control over it. That nothing more could be done. That the medication would wear out and I would be helpless in the agony of suffering. But, when a friend brought me the Toning book and I began groaning and using the breath to hold out the pain, I gained a wonderful confidence that I could do something to control it. Even if I can hold it out for just a few seconds, it gives me comfort."

The power of the voice, with the mind-feeling-breath is a vast, almost unexplored realm in our western culture.

The voice is so important because not only does *it set the pattern of our life, it gives us the use of the will to live it.*

In speaking, Toning or chanting, with knowing and conviction, we are able to bring oneness to our divided nature. We are made whole.

This applies to problems as well as need for healing. When one feels discouraged, inadequate, frustrated, fearful—any negative condition, the transforming change begins the moment one stands up, pulls up the ribcage, breathes deeply and sends the voice out with the authority to correct the condition.

We are the most magnificent creations of which we know. Surely it was intended that we have control over our lives and live in the perfection intended for us; without, of course, causing any harm to another. When one experiences the blessed benefits from Toning, to try to use it in a destructive manner would be unthinkable. Life, which is the moving force of all energy, has a beautiful regulator. It amounts to this: *Whatever is wrongfully used will return to destroy the user.* The voice which embodies feelings of violence, hatred or selfish power will attract those qualities back. Such a one is setting in motion his own self-destruction.

We cannot change the order of the planets about the sun, nor the affairs of the planet upon which we live, but we can move in harmony with the patterns that regulate that energy, and within our own lives become a sun which governs events and circumstances in our private worlds. We were made to identify with the light rather than fight or surrender to the shadows.

"In the beginning was the Word—"

In the end we become the words we speak.

Chapter VI

RESULTS FROM TONING

The pioneer work in Toning has been done by the Fransisters, a group of women, wives, mothers, teachers, professional women, who have met weekly for a period of years to study and serve.

When I first discovered the benefits of Toning in 1960, our little Fransister group had the aspiration to go out and heal everyone in the world. And the world heard about it and came quickly to be healed.

We received requests, by letter and phone, from people in all parts of the country—and miraculous things happened, not only in healing but in other areas. Jobs were found. New clothes arrived. All manner of situations were changed.

But without *the person's own effort to recognize the cause and remove it,* he became as dependent upon our Toning as upon a drug. This is not healing. It may be helpful and comforting, but is considered temporary, as medicine, surgery or other treatment is unless the cause is corrected.

Usually an illness is the result of breaking some natural law, improper diet, emotional upheavals, nervous or physical exhaustion, tensions, etc. And while Toning for them could aid, and relieve pain, the real healing should come from within themselves.

We had to let it be known that we would teach people to Tone for themselves but we could no longer run a first-aid station.

However, in our early experiences we had assurance

that the forces of visualization, feeling and sound, used in Toning could produce remarkable results.

We have been awakened at night to Tone for a stranger a thousand miles away, and relief was reported. We have seen X-rays of the healing of bones (miraculously) when amputation had been considered the only means of saving a life. Certainly the sound does not travel across the miles, or through the earth, yet results are there. We are using some natural force which is not generally recognized yet.

In the beginning, when frowning intellectuals asked me how many control experiments we had done to "prove" this theory, I was happy to reply, "None. We haven't felt the need, nor had the time to waste, to prove something that we find works. We just go ahead and use it."

I do believe that Dr. Tiller has explained how it works in his paper on nodal points extending from a field. "To be in resonance with any one of these points, is to be in resonance with the particular gland of the entity."*

One of our first demonstrations was Toning for a young woman who stopped off in Denver, feeling too ill to continue her plane flight on to New York. She had the flu, a very stiff neck, she was exceedingly weak, not being able to eat for several days, and had a violent headache. As she sat, slumped in a chair before us, she appeared to be a most miserable and helpless person.

Two of us Toned for her for about 15 minutes. I had been standing with my hands, palms together (as in a prayer position) just under my chin. I felt a power build

---

*"Radionics, Radiesthesia & Physics," p. 58. *Varieties of Healing Experience.* Dr. William Tiller, Academy of Parapsychology & Medicine, Los Altos, Ca., 1971.

up in my hands as I Toned and I said to the woman as I walked over and stood in front of her, "Ask what you want but be sure you want it. I feel it will be released to you." (I had never done that before and I was acting entirely on intuition.)

She didn't open her eyes. She mumbled, "I want to be free of this pain and sickness, and whatever caused it—"

I opened my hands and held them, palms out, toward her.

She convulsed in the chair as though she had received an electrical shock.

She sat up and asked, "What happened?"

We could not answer. We stood with our mouths open, too surprised to speak. One thing that I had been taught was "never let fear in, no matter what you are doing." If we could have, we would have been frightened, but we just stood watching.

The woman sat up straight, twisted her head from side to side freely, amazed.

"It's free. No pain. What has happened? I feel wonderful."

Then she stood up, walked about the room and kept saying, "I feel so wonderful. I can't believe it. I don't believe in miracles. This can't have happened, but I feel *wonderful*. There isn't a pain or ache anywhere. I never felt better. And, I'm hungry."

She said she felt as though she were walking on air. We drove her to the airport and while we waited for her plane she ordered a large lunch and ate it all with relish. She kept asking, "What happened?"

We, being new in working with Tone, could only say, "We'll try to find out. We are as astonished as you are."

She told us later that she retained that exalted feeling the rest of that day and night and into the next day, when after working at her office she felt "normal" again. All symptoms of the illness were gone.

What had happened? At that time we guessed that in Toning we had helped her body release the tensions, and it slipped back and rested in its natural pattern. When I opened my hands, whatever power had been built up there, directed to her, caused her consciousness to be instantly aware of her union with her inner perfection. The results were unexpected, and we were convinced that in Tone there was more power than we had dreamed. It was ours to use, to direct—it was within each person to use for himself as well as for others.

A dentist had a biopsy of an unhealed condition in his lip and found it positive. He made arrangements to have radiation treatment and plastic surgery. But, because the holidays came up and he was very busy, he postponed the treatment for 6 weeks. In the meantime his wife Toned for his condition and he Toned with her, to humor her, because he was quite sure it could do no good.

Within 10 days a scab fell off with tiny hair roots, shriveled, still attached to it. It was as though it had been dried up from the tips of the roots, outward, and "died" from the vibration of the Toning. No treatment was necessary. No scar was left. No recurrence of it after 6 years.

Another case of skin cancer was that of a woman who had received radiation treatment for it. When it recurred in the same area less than two years later, she Toned. She said that she Toned "violently," causing a resonance to be set up in the area and continued doing it for 30 minutes at a time for several days. After the first day she said the flesh became swollen and red and had every appearance of having had radiation. "It looked just as it had when I had X-ray treatments." Within a week it was normal again. No recurrence. No other treatment was needed.

A remarkable case was that of a nurse who came to visit her sister. She had lost much of her sight and could no longer read nor drive her car. She had been a diabetic for years but because of uremic poisoning could no longer take medication for it. Multiple sclerosis was becoming apparent. She had come to Denver to say goodbye to her family because her doctors could give her no hope for living beyond a few months, and being a nurse she realized the gravity of her condition.

Her sister brought her to see me. She came up the steps, weakly halting at each one, as though she should have been carried in on a stretcher instead of having only the support of her sister's arm.

She fell into a large chair and seemed to melt into it with her pain and hopelessness.

I talked with her for about a half hour, trying to explain Toning, which wasn't easy. Her mind had long been schooled to strict scientific terms. It would be expecting too much to think that I could convince her that anything we could do in a few minutes with our voices could be stronger or more effective than all the known scientific helps, which now had failed. She listened, politely, or perhaps out of exhaustion, and did not protest.

Then her sister and I Toned for her. We Toned for about 20 minutes. We watched her body react as it might have to very mild electrical stimulation. She sat up straighter—a glow began to come to her white cheeks. Then she began to cry.

She cried, great heart-breaking, shaking sobs which

were a kind of groaning, really. We encouraged her to cry and we went on Toning.

She said, between the sobbing, "Oh, how I have mistreated my body! I never thought about it except why wouldn't it do more, overworking it, hating when it wouldn't go on serving me. Forgive me, God—forgive me!"

This was a surprising outburst because she was not a religious person and would not ordinarily have spoken in such a manner. But in the cleansing of the sound, something was released and the healing could begin. Through the crying and in the realization of how she had mistreated her body, and in asking for some power greater than her own to "forgive," she had loosed something held by her subconscious mind.

I took her hands and drew her to her feet, telling her to rise and stand in the new life that had been produced in her.

She did, and she walked around the room with me, briskly, still crying, and then laughing and proclaiming that she felt so much stronger. She walked down the steps unassisted and got into her sister's car without help. I watched, wondering if this would last, or if she would lose it.

Her sister, with whom she was staying, taught her to Tone and for the few days of her remaining visit, they did a good deal of it together.

The woman did not lose her "healing." She continued to Tone when she returned to California. First, the uremic condition cleared up. Her vision improved. She could drive her car again, and read. The multiple sclerosis not only was halted but diminished over the months.

She went to her hospital for tests to be sure that this healing was fact and not a temporary thing. The doctors could not believe it. They had no explanation for it. The facts were that she was free of certain of her ailments and improved in other areas.

Four years later only the diabetic condition remained and that was controlled by medication. She found new enthusiasm in helping build and furnish a mountain cabin. Beyond the physical helps, she had found a new appreciation for her body, and her mental attitude was changed so that she became a much happier person.

Toning is not "faith healing." People who do not believe in it, or do not know that it is being done for them, respond. Plants and animals respond to it. Certainly, they are not using faith. Toning is the right use of natural laws, as in electricity and nuclear power.

A teacher, whom we knew, had suffered a pain in his right arm and shoulder for weeks. In spite of medication it continued to grow worse. (His physician had not been able to diagnose the condition and more tests were to be taken.) It had made it impossible for him to write on the blackboard or raise his arm above his head.

We Toned for him, without his knowledge. That evening he was called and asked how he felt.

"The oddest thing happened today," he replied. "For no reason that I know of my arm felt better. I could write on the board, something I've not been able to do for a long time. I can't understand it. The pain is just gone. It's just a little sore but not stiff."

The soreness disappeared within a week and there was no more trouble with the arm. This young man was a very intellectual person and if he had known that we were trying to "heal" him, we were sure that his mind would have rejected it. Since he did not know, he was helped. That is "anti-faith" healing, perhaps?

Then there is the case of the rancher who had "tried

everything" and phoned in desperation from Lancaster, California. He had a history of migraine headaches once or twice a week but this one had lasted five days and he was exhausted from the pain. Someone had told him about Toning and he said he was ready to try anything.

"Do you mind the long distance phone bill?" I asked.

"Take as long as you like—just let me get some relief," he answered.

Headaches are difficult to treat because the sound must be soothing or it can accentuate the problem. Since I did not know this man and had never heard from him before, I had to proceed with all of the sensitivity and alertness possible.

Visualization is half of the Toning process. One must reach the subconscious mind with an acceptable impression.

I told the man, "There is an old, inherited body-memory of helplessness when blood drains away from it. Use this imagery now. Imagine that you are a bottle, turned upside down, the cork at your feet. Reach down and imagine that you remove the cork and the blood begins to drain out through the bottom of your feet— *feel it*. Feel that you are helpless to stop it. Feel the pain drain away with it—it is slowly draining down from your head, out through your feet—feel it, feel it." (One of the benefits of this is that the attention is put at the other end of the body!)

"Let your breathing slow down—sigh with each breath —let the tensions drain away through your feet—relax— sigh—let go—sigh. Now, groan."

I listened to him, encouraging him to groan more deeply. I groaned with him. "Deeper—louder—sigh," I urged him. And while he listened to the Tone, my voice gently "massaged" his field. I gave an example of letting the voice rise up after feeling the satisfaction of groaning, and soaring free *above* the pain.

When I felt that he had comprehended the process and was able to do it, I told him I would go on Toning for him, while he did it for himself, and we would anticipate complete freedom from the old pain pattern. By this time he felt his headache beginning to subside a little.

"Don't be afraid if you feel a headache coming," I warned him. "Just start groaning. Pull the cork from the bottle and know it will drain away before it can establish itself." (Fear of an approaching migraine causes more tension and hastens the process.)

Two weeks later he wrote a letter: "Everyone at our house is Toning. Even the coyotes who visit our pastures before sunrise in their quest for unwary and foolish ground squirrels. Yes, they tone, and beautifully.

"Last Wednesday your tape arrived with the Toning example. It was so calming to listen to. I can't recall when we were so relaxed. Our tensions quickly melted away. Now that we've learned the correct way to groan and to Tone we are feeling better each day. For two weeks my usual migraine has deserted me. And I feel it is going to be a permanent divorce.

"I passed the information on to Bill, who works for us. He complained of having painfully clogged sinus cavities. His ear ached and his throat hurt so much that he could hardly swallow, plus his glands down one side of his neck were swollen and so painful he couldn't touch that side of his face.

"He had serious doubts that my advice about groaning would help his trouble. In fact, he said his doctor had told him to 'hum' to open up his sinuses but instead of clearing them, it had plugged them up!

53

"I insisted he give it a try. He said he would and went off to attend to his work.

"At lunch he joined us and gleefully reported that he had been Toning while on the tractor and his nose started draining and his sinus cavities no longer pained. He had no earache and his throat and neck had stopped hurting and he was delighted. So were we.

"My wife joins me in sending you thoughts of gratitude." T. H.

Six months later he felt very confident of his freedom from migraines. He phoned me not long ago to say that during a tension-filled episode in business he felt the old migraine habit starting up but he conquered it quickly and that there has been no recurrence.

Women may find it easier to find time to Tone than men, but there is always a way.

An electrical engineer working on outerspace projects, one who is in the most modern and foremost fields of scientific exploration, is an ardent Toner. He gives this explanation: "Every morning, and I mean every morning, as I drive to work, I Tone. One benefit is the fantastic workout the lungs receive. Toning actually pushes stale air from the lungs. You get rid of this waste from the lungs without becoming exhausted. Ordinarily to try to exhale and empty the lungs is physically exerting. But, when I Tone it is a slow, steady flow of air, caused by the diaphragm pressure instead of my trying to squeeze it out from outside force. Then the inflow of air rushes in after I exhale. I try to make the feed-back loop of breath and Tone so that my body is completely relaxed and I feel that *it settles* into the Tone. Then I let it ride. Maybe this just lasts for 5 seconds or so but if I can get into that point where I ride on the Tone and it is a steady Tone, it seems that everything in my body and mind is stilled in perfect union and it gives me a sense of great concentration and power.

"I am not aware of exhaling, or doing anything. My body and my mind and the sound are all one and I have the feeling that I am being carried by this tremendous Power.

"Then I run out of air and take another deep breath, but it amazes me how long I can 'ride' on this Tone—quite a long time without any effort at all. If I *tried* to take a deep breath and forced it out I couldn't do it nearly as long and I wouldn't feel the benefit I do from Toning.

"It's like driving a car—you start it, put it into neutral and coast. You coast on the sound and you can go a long way on it. That Toning is the most important thing that I do in the morning. I wouldn't go without it. It seems to build a shield around me and anything negative just bounces off before it gets in to me.

"Even if I feel a little tired, or I'm facing a discouraging problem at work, as soon as I Tone everything picks up. It is a mechanical thing. You can't possibly stay 'down' when you Tone, any more than you can stay on the ground floor if you step into an elevator that goes to a top floor."

Now that bio-feedback has become well known, and the terms associated with it have become popular in our daily vocabulary, it is helpful to be able to say, "go into Alpha when you start to Tone." (*Alpha* is the designation given the brainwaves which register on the electroencephalograph machine as approximately 7 to 13 cycles per second. It is below the usual waking, thinking state of *Beta* which range from 13 to 28, or more. Below *Alpha* is *Theta*, from about 4 to 7 cycles per second, and that is the area that is exciting exploration now since it appears to be the area where deep intuition functions, miraculous healings, etc. *Delta* is approximately 0 to 4 cycles and is deep sleep or unconsciousness.)

I have had the privilege of being tested by Dr. Elmer and Alyce Green at Menninger's and found that Toning produced Alpha waves almost at once. Theta could be reached by deep quietness but I found it extremely interesting that I could also register Theta when I kept my mind "still" but felt an inner enthusiasm; what I termed, "contained anticipation." This may have been touching one of the deeper states of meditation which the Indian yogins experience. It is a deep inner awareness that is greatly sharpened, not by "thinking" but by "being." And, I have noticed at times when Toning for others that this Theta does happen. There is so much yet to be explored and found in these areas of functioning. Nothing we can find in outer space can ever equal the wonders that we may discover in our inner space.

Think of Toning as *release*. First, release of tensions, pressures and blockages (through groaning) which prevent the natural, healthy expression of life forces. Second, release of the vital force contained in one's field, according to its pattern of perfection. We release health from within as a flower is released from the pattern in the seed. We release will power as we release the positive feelings of our highest and best intentions. And, we release hope, confidence, love and joyousness—all of these qualities native to the soul, as we let our voice express its freedom.

Chapter VII

TONING FOR OTHERS

When we Tone for others we begin by doing the daily Toning ritual until we feel in perfect balance. We close our eyes for better concentration and Tone the name of the person, usually using the C chord, repeating three times. We use the C chord as it has been determined that the natural tone range of the human voice is from A below middle C to A above. We hold the idea of the quality of each note as we progress upward.

A—the Absolute, Creative Force undifferentiated—the One.

B—descending into dense form; the animal and plant level of manifestation.

C—*Purification* of that form—the turning point, out of the animal level toward the divine.

D—*Vitality*. Here the human begins to form and vitality is given to it. (Interesting to note that our vitamin D gives vitality, C, an infection fighter, etc., yet these qualities to sound were given thousands of years before we named vitamins.)

E—*Harmony*, a bringing together of the lower and higher natures in peace. It is as "salve to the wounds." Healing.

F—*Formation*. F is said to be the great Tone of Nature. Visualize the perfect form to be manifested. We are reminded that what is visualized while F is being sounded must be perfection. Do *not* see a person in bed with an illness while Toning in F—you will only add power to his illness. See him well, going about his daily life, free of limitation.

G—*Gratitude*. Now that the "new" form has been made, rejoice. Let it live through gratitude. "Gratitude is the highest form of prayer" because it is a release, an out-rushing of positive force, lifting one as it goes.

A—(above middle C) The cycle is completed from the unconscious Life force to conscious union with the inner Potential. It is "one with the Father," in Christian terms. One is consciously raising one's "self" from the imprisonment in animal instincts, habits, fears, etc., to a masterful and happy direction of his life.

This cycle of Toning, followed with the visualization as given, is a daily lifting and conquering. It is re-living the traditional story of consciousness "falling" into lower-state functioning, then the purification and return to full potential of human achievement, and joy.

As sleep is said to be the "little daily death," so does Toning in this manner give a pattern of the "little daily resurrection;" taste of immortality.

A psychiatrist told me, "The basic urge in the human is to worship. This urge is deeper than the sex urge, it is experienced from the infant stage to the very aged. The human must look to something greater than he is, something in which he can feel secure because he believes it to be right, changeless, wise, powerful and eternal. He must have such a Power to trust or he does not have an urge to progress. To cut off this need to worship is like cutting the main root of a tree. It then becomes top-heavy and falls. So will mankind become over-mentalized and fall if he does not sustain himself with the nourishment of worship." But worship in its complete sense is to have union with that which is worshipped. For full satisfaction we must DO something to become worthy of, to be similar, to be "one with" the worshipped.

By Toning this cycle daily one assures his subconscious mind that he has control of his life and he *can* change his imperfections. He can lift himself to better living—*he is doing it* by lifting his voice from A to A. It is a symbol *experienced*. It is a conviction to his subconscious mind because it is something he can *feel*.

To be sure we are hitting the note accurately, we use a small chromatic pitch instrument. (It is about the size of a thin yo-yo and we carry it in our pockets and use it frequently during the day.)

Toning the name of the person in "C" chord is first, purification, the "E" healing, then gratitude "G" (acceptance) that the healing is already at work. We seldom Tone for a person more than once. If it is done properly, once should be enough. We who are sensitive seem to have a type of sonar which causes us to "know" when the person has been reached and is healed. Time after time in our little group, we will Tone for some person and then we will ask what each one felt about the person. The majority receive the same impression. I have been asked to Tone for people about whom I knew nothing, not even the nature of the illness. In Toning this sonar system has been verified in enough instances to make me believe it could not possibly be coincidence.

We are not doing a miraculous thing in Toning. We are simply relaxing the person into his natural state of health. Toning may only be the removal of whatever obstruction has crept into the person's "field."

It must be recognized that illness is the result of some discord in the field, and we should look for the cause.

"When an illness comes we know that it is a time when the Father tenderly gathers us closer to Him to tell us something we have been doing wrong, or need to correct, or learn. Sometimes we grow so busy (we think) that we forget how much we need the Grace of union with our divine nature.

"Someone calls and we rush to answer, and another and another, and without realizing it we find that God has been calling and we did not hear Him in the multitude of sounds.

"Then He draws us close, through what we call a problem or illness. And, we listen. In illness, we are forced to listen; to take time to re-evaluate our lives and to sort out the important from the superfluous. Were it not for these periods we might not begin to unfurl the tight little leaves of our spiritual potentialities," so wrote the Founder of the Fransisters.

Each of us can feel secure only when we know that we need not rely upon any outside agent—by releasing the Life within us, are we healed. That is why we encourage the practice of daily Toning.

An amusing example of the old saying, "God will help you out of a difficulty once, but if you repeat the mistake, you'll have to get out by yourself," occurred in our group.

One of our Fransisters knew how to Tone and had healed many minor ailments but she did not pay attention to warning signals of overwork and she contracted pneumonia. Strong medication was administered, and with Toning, she recovered quickly.

The next year, after a similar period of overwork, there were signs of pneumonia recurring. The same medication was ineffective. She was forced to rely upon Toning.

She managed to get out of bed, and as she stood gasping, she began to Tone. She said it was like "pulling her will up by its bootstraps," but up it came. Two hours later she was able to drive out into a snow storm to keep an appointment; and that was the end of the illness.

We do not suggest such drastic self-treatment for beginners. *Do not depend upon what you have not proved.* This is mentioned only as an example of how we may grow careless and repeat mistakes, and are jerked back to proper functioning.

In other ways than illness, Toning is very effective.

A Landlord rented a house to some people who falsely represented themselves and when they were given notice to move, they caused a great deal of trouble and threatened a lawsuit. He did not argue with them. He went home and Toned. He saw them out of his house and going to a place better suited for them. "What is good for one is good for all concerned," is the proper attitude for Toning in such situations.

When he went back to the house 3 days later he found that they had moved. Nothing more had been said to them. Perhaps Toning "gave them an idea" that they did not want to stay and go through the unpleasantness of legal action.

Another case was that of a teacher whose behavior had been considered detrimental to students. For 4 years parents had signed petitions and tried to have the teacher removed. He had tenure. He would sue the schoolboard, he said, for prejudice and other false claims.

A mother, moving into that community and feeling that her children were going to be deprived of their proper education, began Toning.

She Toned, seeing the teacher's chair empty. That was all—no resentment, no anger—just that his chair was empty and that he was drawn to a place where he would be happier, for surely no one could be happy where he knew he was not wanted.

In the middle of the school year, about a month later, the teacher suddenly announced that he was "fed up with the West" and he was going back to civilization in the East. And, he left.

Toning does work. It is not manipulating people, or exerting power over people—the idea is simply to restore people to their harmonic patterns.

Frequently I am the most surprised at the results from Toning. I expect miracles, but what form they will take I do not guess.

I was invited to speak to a group of patients at a mental hospital near Denver.

"Do not be dismayed if there is no response," I was told. "This is a group of chronic cases which have been under treatment for from three to five years. We try to get them to relate to outside interests, but so far they have not responded to group therapy or any of our standard methods."

To get some idea of other subjects they had had I inquired what their last guest had used as a topic.

"We had an official of the telephone company explain dialing and how messages are relayed." (What that had to do with mental health I couldn't imagine, but I did not think it was an act that would be hard to follow.)

I had spoken to inmates at the State Prison, and heard the gates clank behind me in the psychiatric ward at Colorado General Hospital when I went there to speak, and remembered one of the patients saying as I left, "Can't we have her again? I could understand *her*." Whether that was complimentary or not it gave me confidence for this encounter.

I passed patients sitting in the parlors and in the halls,

slouched over, cigarettes or coke bottles in their hands, eyes on the floor—waiting. Waiting for something to happen to make life worth living again.

About twenty-five men and women were seated in a circle in a large room. That was my audience. Two white-uniformed attendants were in the back of the room. I was introduced. No one cared who I was or why I was there. They sat, shoulders bent, eyes staring at the floor.

To get past their mental shells I knew that I must reach the subconscious mind—touch some remembered experience with absurd picturization. I began telling very corny jokes about myself. A head or two came up and eyes looked at me. I seemed to be having such fun that they smiled back at me. Soon there were more heads raised and more smiles. There was interest. It had taken a full twenty minutes out of my allotted hour and a half but it was encouraging. I was using my voice as a lever to pry them up!

I introduced them to groaning. They liked it and a great jumble of sounds began to come out. An attendant disappeared and returned with two more personnel. By then I had the patients on their feet and we began Toning. They were responding! All except one woman who grabbed her coke bottle and walked out defensively.

While they sat down to rest after our vigorous Toning I explained to them, "We make the mistake of identifying with our thoughts. We think our thoughts are reality. They are made of dream stuff. You can't be satisfied by *remembering* eating last Thanksgiving's turkey if you're hungry. It's not real. Memories aren't real, we just think they are. We forget that WE ARE THE THINKER AND WE CAN CHANGE OUR THOUGHTS. And, if we can change our thoughts, and feelings, we can change our world because we make our own world out of memories and opinions and thought-stuff."

A doctor interrupted. "Isn't that being unrealistic? Isn't that rather a Pollyanna approach?"

"What was wrong with Pollyanna? She was happy, wasn't she?" I countered. "Of course we fool ourselves in almost all sense-perceptions. We see the sun rise at a certain time and it hasn't 'risen' at all. We have turned towards it. We hear the sound of a plane in one place in the sky and see the plane somewhere else, where it has traveled before the sound reached our ears. But, let's have sense enough to fool ourselves happy instead of sad. It's our life. Let's make it fun." I spoke in such simple terms for the patients' benefit.

I asked the patients to close their eyes and feel the chairs upon which they were seated, so they could describe them to me if I asked. When they opened their eyes again I told them, "You thought that the chair was smooth, and cool, because that is how you thought it felt. But you didn't feel the chair. *You felt the feeling* in your hand; that sensation triggered a memory in your brain and you *thought* the chair was smooth or cool. The smooth-cool was in your brain, wasn't it?"

Obviously, some of them could not grasp it but I kept trying. "Now, compared to very fine silk that chair would seem rough, wouldn't it? Compared to dry ice, that chair would feel warm, wouldn't it? You see, things are not fixed—not just one way; they are only what *you* think they are. You are the THINKER, not the thought, and you can change your thoughts about—anything. You are the boss of your mind. Make it serve you and do what you want it to do. Now, let's think we're going to have fun."

I got them on their feet, again, and we did an Indian

dance which is stomping and shouting a lot of "Hi-ya, hi-ya-hi-ya, HI," sounds. We were behaving as children, and having a good time.

I looked at the several doctors and attendants in the back of the room. I couldn't resist inviting them to join us—and they didn't dare refuse! It was so comical to see them, too, marching along like Indians, yelling and stomping. We did it until we were breathless and most of the patients were laughing with me.

Many of the patients crowded around me, asking me when I could come back again. "Tomorrow?" they suggested. They liked it.

One man, probably in his late thirties, took my hand and looked me squarely in the eyes and said, "You have changed my life today. I've made institutions a way of life because I thought the outside world was just too tough for me. Today, when you made me see that I am the 'thinker and not the thought' I got the feeling that I can't waste any more time. Maybe life is a game that I'd enjoy playing. Thank you, and God bless you."

"Good," I told him. "Get in there and play to win."

Six months later I was invited back. This time there wasn't a doctor in sight. (They must have heard that I was coming?)

I asked the attendant who was directing me to the right room, "Is this the same group to whom I spoke last time?"

"No," she said brightly, "they have gone into cottages now. This is another group."

They had "graduated" into cottage living after one Toning session? However, there was more to it than that. When I had been there before I had asked how much physical exercise they were given each day, and had been told, "Once a week we have a twenty-minute exercise period."

I must have shown my astonishment clearly. "But they need healthy bodies for restored minds."

I had suggested at least that much exercise every day, with additional singing, folk dancing, interpretative danc-inng—anything that would combine movement and voice and move them out of those dull ruts of just sitting and talking or thinking about their problems. Such a program had been instituted and undoubtedly it had contributed to the patients' improvement.

"Do you remember the man who talked to you the last time you were here?" the nurse asked.

"Yes. Will I see him today?"

"No, he has left us. That is the message he wanted me to give to you. He has a position now. He is a physicist, you know. He wanted me to tell you how much you had helped him, and that he is 'winning.'"

If only one mind had found its freedom from its self-imposed imprisonment, it had been more than worth the effort I had put forth that day. It was another miracle from Toning.

When we become aware of our voice and its influence on other people, we realize that the person who speaks in harsh, bellicose tones causes hostility to flare in return. One who speaks from weakness invites imposition and endless problems. A person who speaks with considera-tion and kindness finds a similar response from others. Most of all, *as we speak we influence ourselves.*

Chapter VIII

MIRACULOUS HEALINGS

Every living thing has its pattern of perfection upon which it was formed. The grass seed, the fruit, the flower, the pattern of the bird in its egg, and man — all have their patterns.

It is natural, therefore, to be healthy and happy. If there are malformations or disease it is an indication that something has disturbed the pattern. Healing is a matter of removing the debris, or coating, which hinders the natural flow of light expanding outward from the nucleus. Today scientists are studying the DNA factor, the inherited pattern within the cells of the body. Their studies have led them into the experimentation with sound vibrations and cellular reactions.

Dr. William Tiller defines one aspect of healing which explains to me how sound vibrations, such as Toning, "loaded with an image" can be effective.

"A basic idea in radionics is that each individual, organism or material radiates and absorbs energy via a unique wave field which exhibits certain geometrical frequency and radiation-type characteristics. This is an extended force field that exists around all forms of matter whether animate or inanimate. A useful analogy here is the physical atom that is continually radiating electromagnetic energy in the form of waves because of its oscillating electric dipole moment and its thermal vibrations . . . Regions of space associated with a given phase angle of the wave constitute a three dimensional network of points in resonance with the particular gland of the entity. The capability of scanning the waveform of the gland exists for the detection of any abnormalities. Likewise, if *energy* having the normal or healthy waveform of the gland *is pumped* into any of these specific network points, *the gland will be driven in the normal or healthy mode.* This produces a tendency for its structure to reorganize itself in closer alignment with the normal structure; healing of the gland occurs. Cells born in the presence of this polarizing field tend to grow in a healthier configuration which weakens the original field of the abnormal or diseased structure and strengthens the field of the normal or healthy structure."* (The italics are mine.)

It was believed in the ancient Mystery Teachings that the nucleus of every human cell was formed around the seed atom which was Spirit and in that nucleus was contained the pattern of its perfection.

Healing meant the release of that perfection so that it was evident in the body.

There was another factor which was associated with that fire of the Spirit. That was Will. Will was divine. It was life. It was God. In western religious writings we are reminded often of the "will of God," and "The Father's Will," and the free will which apparently causes all of our problems.

Will was the spirit of God which moved life into manifestation. It was the activator in creation. If it operated unhampered, all was as it should be and peace resulted.

But back there somewhere when the divine consciousness (image-making ability) came into the animal form, the sensations of the animal nature began to steal the

---

*"Radionics, Radiesthesia and Physics," p. 58, *Varieties of Healing Experience.* Academy of Parapsychology & Medicine, 1971.

imagination process and use this power of the will separate from the instinctive governing factors of the animal nature.

The subconscious mind gained control of the will and held it jealously for through it, it had greater power. Referring to the soul-mind-body relationship, the body now controlled the mind with the willpower it had usurped from the soul, and separated the body's functioning from the soul's direction. Authority had shifted and chaos resulted.

We see the picture of the animal nature which has stolen the power without having the ability to use it wisely, and so would misuse it and destroy itself. (Our discovery of atomic energy is a comparable analogy. New and enormous power came into our use but we have lacked the wisdom to use it properly and we live in danger of annihilation.)

To objectify it we may visualize a chimpanzee which stole the keys to the car of its keeper. By imitating things it had seen the keeper do, it started the car, drove it at full speed until it crashed. Then, sitting bewildered and possibly hurt, it looked back and sought the help of its keeper.

To live in health and peace we must convince the subconscious mind to let the Keeper operate our vehicle. We must loosen its hold on willpower.

Since it has control of our willpower it follows that the "stolen will" must be relinquished back to the Perfect Will for healing to manifest.

This requires the feeling of surrender. But it must be understood that the surrender is to the Perfection and *not to the illness*.

So often people who are ill and hope for spiritual healing will say, "I have surrendered to God's Will." God's Will could never be anything but perfection. They surrender—but to the disease or problem instead, becoming. resigned and negative about it.

A beautiful example of proper surrender is that of a young woman who was told that she had cancer and without surgery could live only a very few months. She had a small baby and 2 other youngsters — and, a religious conviction that God would heal. She resisted the pleas of her husband, family and friends, even her minister, to have surgery. "I stood naked in my faith and utterly alone but I was convinced that God would heal me and if He wouldn't I didn't want to live. I never *felt* doubt."

Her surrender was not to the illness but to the perfection of His Will. Even when she was so ill that she could spend only short periods out of bed she felt that the healing was happening underneath the pain.

All during the summer she kept that lonely vigil of faith and on Thanksgiving day a violent physical reaction occurred. "There was an emptying, a cleansing of my body from the bowels and mouth," she wrote, "which seemed to leave me absolutely hollow and filled with light. It was the most vile, awful stuff that came out, but as soon as it stopped I began to feel stronger and well."

I have her letter written just before Christmas of that year, containing a copy of her doctor's report. "After extensive laboratory tests, we find no cancer cells present—" That, she wrote, was the Father's Christmas present to her.

That was four years ago and a recent letter stated that she is enjoying excellent health.

Her surrender was total but it was to the image of health in which she had been created. She identified with that image. Each day she thanked God for healing. A common misunderstanding of prayer is that when we pray *for* something to come to us, or to happen to us, we are causing the subconscious mind to *acknowledge separation from it*. And that which we seek is held out and away from us. That is why reference is made in the Bible to "pray with thanksgiving." Pray as though what is sought *is already here*. This programs the subconscious mind to accept that image instead of the picture of the lack.

I do not encourage anyone who has any fear or doubt to follow this young woman's example but I do want to relate the case because it can happen, it does happen when the conscious mind completely convinces the subconscious that its true nature is perfect.

Not all people who claim to have faith are healed and this is the source of so much anguish. Why doesn't it work for everyone who tries it?

I have attended gatherings of thousands where the people came in wheelchairs, on crutches, in desperation, believing, trusting and having faith. Out of 5000 people perhaps 80 or 100 were healed. That is a very small percentage, it seems, for an all-loving and powerful heavenly Father to heal. Surely, more than that number believed that they had faith. A human parent does not say to his children, "You will be healed, but you I will not heal; you must continue to suffer," when the child cries out for his help.

This cannot be explained away as divine whim or as a divine mystery that "we are not supposed to understand." I believe that we *can* understand it. At least we must make the effort to find answers.

Even more puzzling to the faithful is the fact that many unbelievers are healed at such meetings. A typical example is one which I witnessed where two women whom I knew attended. One had a slight diabetic condition, the other had a severe arthritic condition in her knee. The diabetic went out of curiosity. It didn't occur to her to ask for healing because she hadn't thought about it happening to her. She was occupied with thinking of a relative whom she should have brought because that person might have been healed. She was completely unconscious of herself. Suddenly "something like a mild shock" went through her and the Evangelist on the platform looked down her way and said, "Three women have been healed of diabetes. Go to your doctors tomorrow and have tests. You have been healed." Later she did go and there was no trace of diabetes.

The girl with the faith, an ardent believer who had dedicated her life to spiritual service, had prayed fervently. Nothing happened. She still has her stiffened leg.

Miraculous healings are not outside of natural law, only outside of man's limited understanding. They are evidence, rather, of the powers available to us which most people do not know how to accept.

While I have been writing this script a woman phoned to tell me of the "miracle" in her life. She had come to see me a couple of months before. She was in her middle thirties and much too young for the arthritis which was afflicting her arms and hands. Her story suggested why it might have appeared. She had been a professional pianist but her husband (a second marriage which she felt must not fail) objected to her playing. He had a violent temper, she said, and criticized her about everything she did, including keeping house and caring for the children. She became depressed, ill, had terrible headaches and spent much of her time in bed.

We had a Toning session and I explained to her how to vitalize her field with hope and enthusiasm, and to use her voice in a positive manner instead of the negative tone. I had heard nothing from her until this phone call.

"I can't believe the change in our lives. I never said

a word to my husband but I began practicing what you told me. I felt better. My headaches stopped. I began to play again and enjoy my housework and last night my husband came in and said, 'I don't know what has changed you but you are certainly a different girl. It's a joy to think of coming home to you at the end of the day. You're so bright and cheerful and you're baking again and making a real home for the kids and me.' "

She finished by saying, "I've been a Christian all of my life and prayed, but until you explained things to me I never knew *how* to let the Father's Will work in my life."

Why does a miracle touch some lives, and not others?

It appears that whether the healings result from Christian beliefs, Indian sand paintings, Shaman's rituals, in Hindu temples or Sufi, for the most part they have two things evidenced. Sound (music, singing, chanting or vocal prayers) and body movement, (clapping, dancing, stomping, kneeling, etc.). A powerful field of psychic or kinetic energy is built up by the audience, or person. Static electricity can be built up in fabric during a wind storm— touching a doorknob after walking across a rug can give an electric shock. *The field is there. Contact with it releases the power.*

When this happens in the body we call it a miraculous healing.

Some may be skeptical and declare such healings are mass hypnotism or hysteria. It is much more than that. In the sense that all healings, as all beauty, harmony and love, are of divine origin, it is creative force in form.

This energy lies latent in all people. (In the cell pattern.) Seldom is it given opportunity to be expressed because the conscious mind blocks it with doubt or denial and the subconscious, through its blind urges, fear or old traumatic experiences, bars the door to its release.

Many of the people who attend healing meetings go as a last resort. They have tried many other types of treatment and experienced repeated disappointments. The subconscious holds those memories. It does not want to be fooled again with vain hopes. It will not be convinced. It will not surrender its will to some uncertain authority again. It reacts from memory. It knows what *has* happened. It cannot imagine what has *not* happened. So, the trusting person with faith, perhaps faith beyond a mental conviction, can't unlock the hold that the subconscious mind retains.

In the case of the two women: The one who was healed was not doubting, she was only curious. Curiosity opens wide the door of the mind. Feeling-wise she was not involved so she was not rejecting it. Her subconscious had nothing to fear. She was wishing her relative were there. In that charged atmosphere where loud singing had gone on for 2 hours and the frequency had been raised with anticipation, excitement and enthusiasm, her conscious mind was totally removed from herself (she was thinking of someone else) and her subconscious mind was overpowered by the energy field. It relaxed—and the Pattern of Perfection was released in a healing.

This is one of the reasons that praying for another often permits our own prayer to be answered. We catch our subconscious off guard and the Divine Will takes control.

Another instance of this is that of one of our young Fransisters. In her mid-thirties an arthritic spine promised no future but a wheel chair. Pat had a baby and two other small children, but even with her affliction she could not resist helping others who had "greater afflictions"— of having no faith or spiritual awareness. She took a girl into her home to help. The girl had an unbelievable

74

background, beginning in the slums where she had to fight to live—for bread and for her body. Pat was the first person she had found who loved her and asked nothing in return. Just loved her. She was nursed back to health and self-respect and a bright future was ahead.

When the time came for the girl to leave, with her new husband, she came to Pat to thank her and say goodbye.

Pat wrote, "I had found that Toning could help me live with pain. While I was Toning, and for a short time thereafter, I would have a 'breathing spell.' Jean had come in while I was kneeling, Toning. We had Toned for ourselves and others. We had now entered our quiet time of meditation when we sought guidance, grace, courage, peace, whatever was needed to fill the perfection of our souls.

"Suddenly, I began to experience a strange sensation. I felt as though I was in a vortex of violent whirling. It seemed that every atom of my body had joined with the other atoms and that they all were whirling at a terrific speed in something of a spiral going around and up. I cannot say how long this lasted. I was not dizzy, yet I could not have moved. I knew that whatever was taking place within or upon my body was good. But, I could not comprehend what was happening.

"Then I knew! As the whirling sensation was going up and up, each joint was giving its pain into the whirl of light. What was left was the feeling that each joint was now resting upon a cushion of air rather than grinding bone against bone. An unbounded joy began to fill me.

"The whirl was still going. I tried my voice, not sure that it would work. It did. I didn't attempt to open my eyes or even to move. 'Jean' I said, 'the most extraordinary thing is happening to me.'

75

" ' What?' came her tense reply.

"As best I could I tried to describe the sensations taking place inside of me. If my joy was great, hers was greater.

"She told me that she had been pouring out her feelings to God. She told Him how she felt such a burden on all of us and how desperately she wanted to offer something in return for the new life she had found through us. She prayed not for herself but that God would somehow relieve my pain. In her wildest dreams she had not hoped for what actually took place. But her deep emotional feeling, apparently lifted me up to freedom.

"When the whirling sensation had abated, we both thanked the Father for His perfection working out in all things and *I stood up*. That sounds like a small thing but for me it had become a slow and painful exercise in discipline. Not this time. I stood up effortlessly, every joint moving on its cushion of air. I experimented. I bent down. Flexed muscles that had been idle for days because the joints to which they were tied had become immovable. The baby toddled to me, expecting me to pat her head as she hugged my legs, for it had been a long time since I could lean down to cuddle her.

"Now, I leaned down, snatched her up and danced around the room. She chortled with surprise and glee. There is simply no way to describe such sudden freedom, the release that comes after being imprisoned within one's own body.

"I tell myself that there must be some concise sentence that would tie this story all together and end it, but the miracle has not ended. It continues each day."

Chapter IX

DOES TONING ALWAYS WORK?

The voice releases power. Weight lifters release a loud grunt *before* they lift. A Karate expert gives a sharp cry *before* he strikes. Obviously, sound is related to a release of energy. It is a direction of energy in the body.

Until a person has recognized this power of the voice through Toning practice he may not have use of the dynamo at the central station. If he does not speak from his solar center, he is speaking off the top of his head. There is no life in his words. They dip down into the throat area as into a very shallow dish of water and throw it out in a slight spray of scattered droplets. All that he has to use in speaking is a froth or residue which has been forcibly squeezed out and left over from its source, the body-voice, and it is a dead husk.

Every student will remember how he has sat through long, dry and boring lectures given by a professor using this type of voice. Nothing is remembered. Nothing has been given to remember because the professor's mind was a bachelor and not having contact with the subconscious mind (feelings), no new thing was born.

In contrast, there is the speaker who sets his audience afire with enthusiasm and new ideas. Using feeling, he has the power to move others because he has impregnated the "mother" in the subconscious minds of his audience so that they will give birth to his ideas.

This is the danger of listening, passively, receptively to impassioned activists. They can hypnotize the minds of their listeners to do what good judgment would deny.

77

Hypnotism is only the process of putting the conscious mind aside and going directly into the subconscious and directing it. One may be standing, wide-eyed and awake, or sitting before a TV screen and be completely hypnotized by the speaker's voice. This is true whether it is experienced directly, or as entertainment. Whatever holds our attention has hold of us. If it reaches our feelings, we are involved, and so we give birth in some area of our life to the ideas which we have let enter our consciousness.

Sound is a motivating force. It appears to be creative or destructive as it collects substance in the wake of its movement, much as water takes on patterns after a motor boat passes through it.

To give you a better idea of this, watch the process of releasing sound in your own body. When you have been quiet, eyes closed and very relaxed for a while, think of speaking. Watch the feeling of tightening, or gathering, which takes place in the solar plexus. Your intention to speak stirs there and you will become aware of the energy coming up into the throat and mouth, and producing sound. At least that is how it should be, and will be, when you have practiced Toning for a while. It is the *alive* voice, the mother-voice which gives form and birth to the idea in the mind.

Remember, that the subconscious mind is fascinated by its voice. We hypnotize ourselves daily with repetitious words.

"I am afraid it is going to storm." "I am afraid they won't come." "I am afraid it won't work out." That person conditions himself to be afraid—in time, of everything.

Or, the one who says, "I can't stand cold weather." "I can't stand old people." "I can't stand waiting." Soon, a skiing accident has put a leg in a cast, or arthritic knees prevent standing, or a sprained ankle will relieve the person from standing.

The subconscious mind will follow the instructions given to it, with feeling. It is a sensitive computer. It will feed back what has been programmed into it.

When one has been Toning and feels that the subconscious mind is cooperative, one must be careful of the use of the voice for that very reason. "My word shall not return unto me void."

Some amusing incidents came to me when I began Toning. Unconsciously I used the creative formula of "visualization, feeling and breathing." (Breath here refers to that quick intake, or gasp, that carries the image to the subconscious as a camera shutter lets light onto the film and imprints the negative.)

At a lecture I met an acquaintance and noticed the beautiful amethyst stone in a ring which held her neckerchief. It was beautiful (visualization) and I *felt* a kinship with it, for it is my birthstone, and I gasped with delight, "What a beautiful stone. Where did you get it?" I felt I would like to have one like it.

She told me that she had found the ring in Mexico and liked it because it was her birthstone, too. Then I forgot about it.

Later that night, as we drove home, she rather reluctantly drew the ring off and handed it to me. "I feel that this should belong to you."

I protested, but she insisted that she could get another one when she went to Mexico again.

That ring, dear to me, is a constant reminder—to keep my mouth shut. At least, when I open it to do so with forethought.

A girl who found Toning very easy and a natural thing

to do shared some of her early experiences. One day she went to a shop and saw a beautiful suit which she desired intensely. Her nature was impulsive and her purse impoverished. The price of the suit was $110.00 and she could not afford $10.00 at that moment. But, she "breathed it in" with deep longing. And, went home.

Not too long after that she phoned to me. "It works! You know what? I've got three suits. One came from a relative who outgrew it, another came from a friend who wanted to trade it for some baby-sitting and the other came to me from the people who moved out of the house across the street. They asked me to take their discards to the Goodwill after I'd taken out anything I could use. And in that stuff was a suit, the same color and made almost the same way as the one I saw in the store. Now, how do I stop this suit thing? I don't want any more. I want a new washer and dryer—."

I do suggest that people be fully aware of their desires. A married man who begins to Tone should not look at a beautiful young girl and gasp. He may be paying alimony to three or four in no time at all. And the doting, possessive older woman should not look at a small baby and wish that her own children were "little again." Some of her grown children may suddenly leave their brood with her to raise while they go off to find themselves.

The warning must be reiterated. Be sure that you know what you want, because you are almost sure to get it. It may be delayed. That which you desire at 26 may not arrive until you are 56, when it can be a burden, but it will come. You are operating a natural law, as reliable as gravity. Be certain that you can handle it wisely. You can no longer hide under ignorance and blame other people for what occurs in your life. You realize that you create your own world and environment. You make the choice to direct your life forces, or you make the choice not to (this invites other people to use your life), but it is still your choice.

I have been asked, "Does Toning never fail?"

In some cases where we have Toned for others, the expected results have not manifested. Here again, none of us is wise enough to direct another's life beyond that one's own will. (Nor, should anyone wish to, knowing the results!)

Whenever a person has Toned for himself there have always been beneficial changes noticed.

Some people who asked for help had psychological reasons for holding on to their illness, as the woman who used her heart attacks as power over her husband; the lonely spinster whose only opportunity to receive male attention was to keep her allergies and visit her doctor regularly for shots. Then there was the very old man who lay in a coma for months (until his insurance ran out) and was fed by artificial means and given blood transfusions. In such instances we see each person in perfection and feel that the love sent out with the Tone will be of some use at some time. And, the act of Toning is always advantageous to the Toner!

Outside of miraculous healings, some conditions are of too long standing for total correction, but Toning can help. A lovely young woman with multiple sclerosis, confined to a wheelchair, told me that she received treatments every 4 hours and they were very exhausting and painful to her. But when she found out about groaning, they became endurable. "And it sounds so silly that I can't help laughing, and that is the best of all."

Recently, in a hospital wing where terminal cancer patients are cared for I heard a nurse urging her patient to groan. "Don't hold it in," she said gently. "Go ahead and groan, it will be good for you." How pleased I was to know that this is being recognized as one of nature's reliefs.

Then there is the supposition offered, "Well, if you can Tone and correct every ailment, you could go on living indefinitely."

Most of us know that in living there is also the wish to die. Psychiatrists have long tried to deal with that unconscious "death-wish" in patients.

Even doctors, who often die of the very illness they were noted for curing in their patients, and spiritual healers, carry a growing desire to be free of their work—of the demands made upon them by people, of trying to meet ever increasing needs of others. There is a longing to rest—a deep, powerful urge to escape all that is expected of one. Death is the only real escape that the subconscious mind understands.

It is as though the divine part of the human being wishes to go on serving unselfishly forever but the body part of him, the part that is doing the work, becomes exceedingly weary and wishes to rest in the normal cycle of rest experienced in nature.

The many frustrations, disappointments, and even boredom of meeting the same circumstances over and over, accumulate until they become a load too heavy to carry.

If you do not believe this, just imagine that you had to live right here forever! Looking at the same face in the mirror for eternity? Brushing those same teeth, or the same dentures? Having to be fitted with glasses, stumbling over the split-vision of bi-focals and forever losing your glasses and not being able to find a number in the telephone book or read something handed to you until you could find them? Coping with the ever increasing Christmas card list, and the "numbers system," (telephone numbers, license numbers, zip-code numbers), more and more things to remember? Having to entertain the same people socially, or in business, and eating the same foods, laughing at the same tired jokes? Living with the same set of relatives forever? Even to have to live with yourslf, with your own weaknesses, inadequacies, faults, etc.? You think you aren't secretly longing for the time you can escape all that, and rest?

So while it should be possible to extend one's life time considerably with Toning, no one really wants to live in this realm of pain, taxes, noise, hurry and problems forever. But Toning can, without doubt, make the living here much more pleasant, healthier and useful for as long as one does remain in a physical body. And it can help in the transition when it comes.

A beautiful example of that came to me when a mother of 3 teenage children called me from the hospital. She was there for open-heart surgery. She told me that she had suffered numerous heart attacks and the doctors said that this was the only hope, "but they can't assure me it will be all right. It's a gamble that I must take. I don't mind for myself but I am so afraid to leave my children. What will happen to them?" And she sobbed, "I'm so afraid—."

I put everything aside and went into my little sanctuary to Tone for her. It seemed that there would be little hope for a recovery but there could be comfort. It was a beautiful Toning session and I felt at peace afterwards.

The next day she phoned again. Her voice was calm and beautiful, actually it sounded joyous. "I wanted you to know—it's all right. Yesterday, after I talked with you, I had the most wonderful spiritual experience. I was taken right into Heaven. It was so beautiful—so wonderful—the light and peace—there is nothing like it on earth. I didn't even want to come back here! And I knew that my children were in God's keeping which is wiser and more loving than mine. There is nothing to be worried about. Whatever happens Monday (the day of surgery) doesn't matter to me, now. If it took this suffering and illness to bring me to that blessed experience yesterday, it has all been worth it." She thanked me and gave me her blessing.

On Monday the operation was performed but she never regained consciousness. When I attended her funeral I could feel only a sense of the joyousness she had shared with me. It was as though she were saying, "Don't grieve for me, you people. It is for you who don't know the glory that is possible that I grieve."

A year later I saw her children again. While they may have caused their mother concern while she was here, her influence upon them since death was very marked. They spoke of her with such tender affection and admitted that her presence seemed to be with them all the time.

We may not understand the intricate and mysterious weaving of the patterns in life and death, but we do know that in such instances there can be a state of great peace.

Toning always helps.

TONING TAPES

There are two toning tapes available through Gentle Living Publications, P.O. Box 27522, Denver, CO 80277:

#1   Explanation and Examples
#2   Workshop Excerpts

Please write for ordering information.

Chapter X

BREATHING FOR SLEEP

All aspects of Toning are related to the breath. Breath is life. When we become aware of our breathing patterns we can cooperate with the natural rhythms and have better control of our life.

An important aspect of good health—physical, mental and emotional—is the ability to sleep. Yet it seems that people are finding it increasingly difficult to do this very natural thing because of the pressures and tensions they encounter in daily living.

By changing the breathing pattern it is possible to put one's self to sleep in a matter of minutes.

Many studies are being made of the sleep process. Dr. Nagandra Das, in his research in the subject at the University of Michigan, concluded that the usual procedure of going to sleep requires about an hour of quieting the beta brain waves (rapid thinking activity) down through alpha, theta to delta (deep sleep). It is in delta that the body and mind are restored, so the second hour of sleep is considered the most important. If one retires at 10, the revitalizing period will be from 11 to 12, or 11 to 1. After that dream activities increase and release many of the sense-perceptions which have registered on the brain, usually during the previous 24-hour period.

"The dream mechanism is like shaking the day's dust and trash from the rug," Dr. Das told me. "If the mass of information and sensations that flood in on the brain were not allowed to escape through dreams, the

burden would cause serious psychological complica-
tions." He considered only a small percentage to be
psychologically significant, however. "People try to
find meaning in every dream. That is like trying to find
jewels in the vacuum sweeper's accumulations. Most
dreams are a feed-back of the day's registry. Especially
those that reflect the TV programs that we watch.
People sit before the TV in a passive state, similar to
light hypnosis and the impressions taken in must find
an outlet either through dreams or influencing the
conscious state. I have seen some people so fascinated
by their dreams that they become dream-addicts, waking up several times during the night to record their
dreams. That can be detrimental, in my opinion. It is
disturbing their needed rest. The mind is busy enough
in waking hours, we should not let it dominate our
sleeping, too. If the subconscious has an important
message it will come through a vivid dream but that
type is rare and cannot be ignored."

Since a third of our lives is spent in sleep, and it is so
necessary to our wellbeing, we should not take it for
granted, or as something to do when we have exhausted
other interests.

Sleep should be approached with respect, with anticipation and, because it is a mystery, perhaps with awe.
Certainly we should prepare for it and have the same
delighted expectancy for it as we do for a fine meal. It is
nourishment of a different kind.

Many people consider reading in bed an invitation to
sleep. Some doctors question that. The awkward position of propping the head up with pillows causes strain
on the back and neck as well as eyes. It seems to me to
read before going to sleep is like snacking before going
out to a banquet. It is filling the mind with more

activity. One should be hungry for sleep, and go to it eagerly as to a feast.

It is essential that the body be relaxed and any method that one finds helpful should be used. However, the secret of sleep is in the breathing rhythm.

Listen to the breathing of a baby or someone asleep. They take in little *short breaths with long pauses in between.*

Oxygen is necessary for brain functioning. We work, speak, think and act on the supply of oxygen in the brain.

The waking breath pattern:

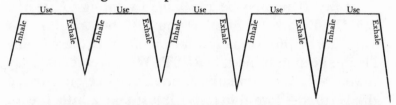

When we exhale, we inhale again immediately and so keep the steady flow of oxygen to the brain. When one is hurrying or climbing, the breathing is faster. When one is lifting something, the breath is held for greater strength. Where ventilation is lacking, one becomes drowsy.

It follows that the sleeping breath pattern is just the opposite. Oxygen supply is diminished. We cannot think without it, so the brain becomes quiet and we slip into sleep.

Sleeping breath pattern:

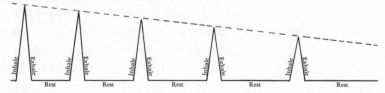

Visualization and feeling accompany the change in breath rhythm.

1. Visualize yourself in a white cloud, or fog. You can see nothing but the soft whiteness around you. You hear nothing. (If there is some noise as there is in any city dwelling, feel that it is receding and will be shut out by the fog.)

2. *Make every breath a sigh.* Let go—tensions, thoughts, breathe them *out.* Begin with large sighs and as you release the breath feel yourself slipping comfortably deeper and deeper into this downy cloud where you float like incense on still air.

At first there may be a feeling of wanting to breathe rapidly. Breathe as often as you wish but *keep the air out. Exhale immediately after inhaling.* If there is any idea to keep in mind it is REST. When you exhale say to yourself, "I can breathe as often as I like but I'm too tired—tired—I want to rest. I'll just take a little breath and then rest—." Inhale, exhale and enjoy the long pause—you are resting.

Let the sighs be audible at first—empty the lungs with little groans. The pauses between breaths become longer and the breathing more shallow. The brain receives less oxygen, the body is relaxed and deep sleep is the natural result.

It has been claimed that if one will keep the mind fixed on the protecting cloud (keeping all thoughts and pictures outside of it) and the feelings upon rest, and use that rhythm of breathing, one cannot stay awake longer than 15 minutes. I have found it true in helping many people go to sleep and for myself I know that even after an exciting evening, stimulated by an audience or lecture, I can put myself into deep and refreshing delta-sleep within minutes. I have never taken a sleeping pill, and if you use this technique I believe you will not feel the need for one either.

Here again we are directing the mind to cooperate with the body's natural functioning. Instead of letting it race about wildly, dragging our attention through mazes of unimportant picture-making, we use it to give the body its rightful restoration.

ECHO

"From the great whirl of Light a spark danced off and in its dance gathered star-dust into form. But the spark was fragmented into pieces of the form and lost its way. And, ever seeks return."

You are a spark. Each of us is a spark.

All of us know from experience that we are happiest when we are serving, feeling useful, doing something worthwhile, releasing that inner fire, or spark, into creative form, letting it find its way back to its natural state.

But, we forget and become lost in the objects of our creation.

By nature we are ego-centric. The world revolves around "me." Somewhere we lost the understanding that it was we who created our private world—by our desires, evaluations, reactions and aspirations. We behave as a sun which comes to look upon its planets for its source of fuel and light, instead of releasing the energy within itself. We look to the world outside for the answers which should come from within.

We expect atomic weapons to be our strength. We look for something outside—a far-away divine power, the government, laws or organizations, to protect and provide for us and do what we should feel capable of doing for ourselves. All these things have a place, but they become detrimental to us if we depend entirely upon such sources and forget to develop our own enormous potentialities.

Power comes from concentrated forces. Sunlight falls upon a sheet of paper and nothing happens, but when the rays of the sun are focused through a magnifying glass, the paper begins to burn. The Laser beam is our recognition and use of such power.

With an understanding of bringing together and focusing the forces within us, through Toning, we can direct these energies to the achievement of which we are capable. We, too, can catch on fire and burn—we can expand that spark, which became so coated and crystallized in its fragmented state, to reunite with its Source.

It is possible to be creative, to change our environment, to be healed, to make life useful and, most of all, joyous. Proper use of the voice is a means of directing the forces in our field to unite with their perfect pattern so that we may function in its harmony and be as wonderful as we ARE. We are the only creatures capable of changing our lives through imagination and will. It is our divine inheritance and we should claim it.

You can create a new world for yourself through the power of your voice.

Let your life sing!

POSTSCRIPT, 1976

Often people have asked if I consider audible prayer to be more powerful than silent prayer. The intensity of feeling has much to do with the efficacy of any wish, but it appears that sound has a definite influence.

There is a story from India that points this out. "If a person in the room wishes me to bring a glass of water and silently requests it, I may not receive the message, but if he speaks aloud I shall respond immediately."

"But, God is not deaf," it was argued.

"Ah, but God is very busy and if I speak aloud, someone is bound to hear and come to my aid."

Sound does set many forces into motion. In a recent paper by Dr. William Tiller* he writes, "If we compare magnetoelectric light (ME) with electromagnetic light (EM) then—for the same wavelength the ME light has a frequency ten orders of magnitude larger than EM light."

It seems reasonable that sound, as light, has subtle frequencies, perhaps not yet recognized, which in the same way are of larger magnitude than previously understood, and it is on them that Toning travels from person to person across space. We may not understand how—but we do know that results are evidenced when Toning is practiced. We stand in the humorous position of the young person who brought some new evidence to a scientific Board for review. A rigid old scientist said, "Young

---

*Positive and Negative Space-Time Frames as Conjugate Systems, Dr. William Tiller, Dept. Material Science, Stanford U., Stanford Calif. '75.

man, if you were educated as we are you would realize that what you have done is impossible!"

We know that fine sand on a drum takes geometric patterns if the drum is placed on a piano which is being played. Sound moves matter.

Recently a grant was given for scientific study of the influence, if any, of silent mental "treatment" on live tissue. The experiments were conducted by a scientist in the research laboratory of a Colorado university, under the usual strict controlled conditions. Practitioners of different faiths attempted to increase cell growth with their various methods. To date, none have had any influence upon the cells. (However, it must be remembered that this experiment was made upon cells taken from living tissue, placed in plastic dishes in an incubator in a laboratory, and were not connected with the consciousness of a living body which might respond in a different manner. There have been many cases of healings reported by such methods so they cannot be discounted.)

Interestingly enough, when sound was introduced to absent treatment, cells *were* influenced. A small group of people using Toning and chanting, along with visualization and feeling, caused the cell growth in the plastic dishes to increase 13%. This group was 25 miles from the laboratory, so it was not sound as we hear it that reached the cells.

When I was given the opportunity to try the experiment I decided to destroy malignant cells taken from a brain tumor. I Toned for 5 minutes, twice a day for 3 days, visualizing the cells changing into light, vanishing. Instead of dying—they grew 6%! That convinced me that "life cannot be destroyed. It changes form or expands in its own pattern." By directing my attention and voice to the cells, I was watering the weeds, and *they grew in their own pattern* which was malignancy. It appears that consciousness focused upon living substance, stimulates it as sunlight upon a plant. Could this be part of the reason that in spite of billions of dollars spent on cancer research, the disease increases each year; that so much attention placed upon it is feeding it?

On my next attempt to influence the cells in their plastic dishes, miles away, I Toned for 5 minutes, twice a day for 3 days, visualizing their expansion and Toning with a feeling of great joyousness. There was a 17% increase in growth. Granted, that is small, but it is evidence that sound produced by the human voice can influence cell growth, miles away. Think what it can do to the cells of our body as we speak or Tone!

From this it seems obvious that to treat disease we should not focus attention and feeling upon it, but visualize and Tone for the healthy, normal cells and let them displace the foreign ones as they become more vigorous and grow in their perfect pattern.

"Speak the word only, and my servant shall be healed," as given in Matthew 8:8 takes on new meaning when we realize that the voice is a vehicle for good, or destruction, as we release its power.

Chants and mantras, as well as prayers, grew out of the human response to release feelings of adoration, worship or supplication. Dr. Judith Tyberg writes in her book, *The Language of the Gods*,* "Primitive language was born from imitating sounds of nature and from vocal expressions responding to physical and vital movements innate with their own essential sound-vibrations.—Every

---

**Language of the Gods*, Dr. Judith M. Tyberg, East-West Cultural Center, Los Angeles, '67.

95

sound in Sanskrit is said to have two aspects, the more audible sound and the subtler essential sound-element behind, vibrant with the meaning natural to it. This vibrant sense-sound within is the real or fundamental sound, called *sphota*. The outward audible sound, its instrument of expression, is called the external sound. The *sphota* arises in the indivisible, permanent Spirit, and is eternally luminous with power and when the spoken word, its vehicle, is perfectly sounded within and without, it stimulates this inner vibrant activity with the result that the power within responds and illuminates."

Performed with this understanding, chants can be very effective. Familiar ones are *Om, Om Mani Padmi Hum,* and *So-Ham*. From Christian origins we have, *Lord, have mercy upon me, Praise the Lord* and *Halleluia*, etc. *Nam Myoho Renge Kyo*, introduced in Japan in the 13th century, is used today in many countries. The Fransisters studied the chants of many religions and found certain rhythms and sounds (such as the "O", "mmm" and "ho") common to most, so they devised one that can be chanted on a chord or to a favorite melody. *One with all life, Holy I am*. It is good to chant as one is doing housework, driving a car, working in rhythm with machinery, almost anywhere and any time. It can be done softly, almost whispered, so long as one is hearing it inwardly. It keeps the mind occupied with the beauty of sound and permits the soul to be free in its communion with its Source.

"I will sing with the spirit, and I will sing with the understanding also."*

Since the first experiments with Toning in 1957, examples of benefits continue to increase. Even I am as-

*1 Cor. 14:15.

tonished at some of the results related to me. The greatest, of course, are felt when one Tones for one's self.

Toning energizes us and gives us confidence that we can control our lives. While we live in a rapidly changing world and are confronted with circumstances not always to our liking, Toning gives us the feeling that we have full authority over our *reactions* to those circumstances.

We can always BE the person we wish to be as long as we are conscious of the creative power within, and attune ourselves to our divine pattern through the practice of Toning.

ADDENDUM, 1982

In the years since 1959 when I discovered Toning I have learned many broader advantages to its use. It has proved to be far more wonderful and beneficial than I had imagined. It has opened up new vistas of understanding about life forces in healing and our relatedness to the world in which we live.

The recognition of the importance of sound is being found around the world. From the All-Union Research Institute of U.S.S.R. comes this statement: "Sonic oscillation, when applied to the human body, will effect a micromassage of tissues and cells which effect a balance and improve blood circulation, metabolism, and the pulsing of the nervous system and endocrine glands."

Dr. Peter Guy Manners at Bretforton Hall Clinic, Worcester, England has done some remarkable work in what he calls "a phonology of vibrations and wave effects, called 'Cymatics.'" He considers Cymatics and the use of sound in medicine and other forms of research to be a very important study of the future. "Experimentation indicates that human beings, as all objects, are radiating sound waves, therefore their fields are sonic fields. Each individual has his own different pattern, or collection of tones just as each individual has a unique shape. We can see from this that harmony is the secret of perfect health. Within the human body any deviation from this harmony would result in ill health. This harmony of sound will only exist within the body providing that each molecule within the body plays its part in the whole. In any deviation, if the molecule is moved or displaced in any way, the general theme of the body's harmonics will be upset."

The purpose of all Toning is to restore the vibratory pattern of the body to its perfect electro-magnetic field, so that it will function in harmony within itself.

Dr. Manners goes on to say, "We can easily see that each organ will have its own sonic (or sound) field. If properly detected this should provide information on processes going on in a particular organ. Since the cells and molecules of the human body are constantly being torn apart and rebuilt, whatever holds them in a constant pattern must not change. If it does, a deformation in its chemical constituents must result. The body, as well as the particular organ, is not a heap of matter accumulated at random but a well organized entity."

That an organ has intelligence and can respond to direction was proved to me by an incident involving a kidney stone.

A gentleman, musical director of a large church and instructor of music at a college, had suffered with a kidney stone all summer. He had been hospitalized a couple of times but the doctors considered its position would not safely submit to surgery. "Wait," they said, "until it moves a little."

The Fall term was approaching and the patient felt quite incapable of meeting his heavy obligations. When I heard about it, I said, "I'll Tone for you. In the meantime let's use everything. Try the Cayce castor oil pack." (Edgar Cayce advocated that for a number of things — a piece of flannel soaked in castor oil applied to the stricken area and covered with a hot water bottle.)

It was about 6 P.M. when I started to Tone and the

100

pack was placed on his back. At 11 P.M. he was taken to the hospital in great pain. The doctors were pleased. The stone had moved.

"Just a little more and we will do surgery," they encouraged him. He was sedated and kept for a couple of days and then sent home since nothing more happened.

I knew him to be a very sensitive person and probably at the first indication of more pain the fear would cause tension and he would unwittingly stop the process.

The next time I Toned I did not tell him. On a Sunday afternoon, after I felt that I had tuned in to his field, I visualized the kidneys and talked to them with firm authority, picturing the process as I Toned and spoke.

"You are going to be cut, mutilated, torn, stabbed — with needles poked into you, if you do not relax and let that stone pass out! The body will be kept in bed with tubes and needles stuck into it and the pain will be terrible and you won't be able to do anything about it. Now — RELAX and let that stone pass and you'll be free of pain. Let it go, let it go — relax — let it pass, and you'll be free."

Early Tuesday morning the man phoned, elated. "Guess what? That stone passed with practically no pain! It is such a pretty little irridescent thing I think I'll have it put in a ring."

Sometimes we have to take command of the body since it cannot understand what may be imposed on it from the outside. When it is given a choice, it will choose the better way. But the process of communication with it must combine strong visualization, Toning, (vibration) and the feeling of acceptance for the subconscious mind to bring about the anticipated result.

When I do lectures I always give a demonstration of how sound can alleviate pain. The volunteer from the audience stands, facing me, about 4 feet away. I scan the body with sound, beginning with a very low note and going up. As with sonar, a problem reflects back to me with a sense of discord, heaviness, stickiness, roughness, etc. Then I send the voice into that area in a pulsating rhythm, directing it to drain away back into the earth. The voice seems to comb the pain out of the person's field and dispose of it.

I demonstrated this recently on a lady who had an intense pain in her shoulder. She exclaimed in complete surprise when I had finished. "It's gone! I never would have believed that sound could take pain away. I am an anesthetist in a hospital and I've never seen anything like this. I'd never have believed it if I had not experienced it."

This brings up the question of why anyone would have to be in pain, become ill or die. There are limits. I am well aware that when I leave this configuration of energy that I call "my body," someone will ask, "Why didn't she heal it? Why didn't Toning work?"

All of us ordinary people go through the experience of withdrawal at some time. The body is of the earth and follows the laws of the earth. It wears out. It grows from conception (or planting of the seed) through nurturing, formation, birth (or appearance) expansion, experience, flowering, fruition—and recapturing all of that process back into the seed for another unfolding in some other springtime.

Some people who are quite fulfilled simply slip out of the form as a hand out of a glove. Others who are very involved with their experiences have to be forced out by the body suffering pain and deserting them.

An old Indian proverb depicts that type of departure.

"If the fruit clings too long to the tree it will become rotten and violent storms of winter will finally tear it loose." Intense pain will convince the consciousness that it no longer wishes to be trapped in that form. It seems rather barbaric and uncivilized to continue that imprisonment by artificial means and technology when the life-span of active, useful self-functioning is spent. *When an activated corpse becomes a burden to itself and others, it is not prolonging life, it is prolonging death.*

A dear friend, Madora Krauzlis, is an example of accepting Sister Death as St. Francis did. In June she was persuaded to consult a doctor because of rapid weight loss although she did not feel ill. The doctor insisted that she go into the hospital immediately for surgery, chemotherapy, radiation — all of the treatments for cancer.

Typical of the manner in which she had moved through her life, always in quiet beauty and the authority of her choices, she replied, "I'll do no such thing. I'll not torture this body that has served me well for 76 years, by pouring poisonous chemicals into it."

She went home. She arranged her affairs, gave away things to people she wished to have them, visited her family, put everything in order and 3 months later, in her own bedroom, she slipped into a coma for a few hours. Holding her husband's hand, she smiled and "breathed out" and left her body. In that terminal illness she had only 3 Tylenol tablets for pain! She left this message: "Cancer can be a friend when you are old and ready to leave. It gives you time to prepare. It is fighting it that causes so much pain. I believe by cooperating with it, as a traveling companion preparing for a journey, suffering is reduced to a minimum."

∽

When we realize the influence of sound as a creative or destructive force on our lives, we may well stand in awe of it. Shu Ching (6th Century B.C.), said, "For changing people's manners and altering their customs there is nothing better than music."

Some 1500 years ago, Cassiodorus wrote in his *Divine Letters*, "Music doth extenuate fears and furies. It can appease cruelty and causeth quiet rest; it cures all irksomeness and heaviness of the soul."

Consider the effect these sounds have upon you: A pleasant voice answering the telephone, a boss's reprimand, a mother's lullaby, thunder in the night, a child's scream, a dog's growl, a mountain stream tumbling over rocks, a bird's song at dawn, an endearment from a loved one, or a church choir singing an ancient hymn.

Almost every moment of our day we are reacting to some sound. Breathing and heartbeat respond to sounds whether we are aware of them or not. Sound probably influences us more than any other sense perception. Usually we become conscious of what we see, but seldom are we moved by peripheral vision. However, even if our attention is focused on some task, when a lively tune is registered by the ears the foot will begin to move. Sound and music control our emotions, actions and moods. Their power is even greater because we are not discriminating about it. We subject ourselves, passively, while we accept it as entertainment. Few have understanding of the benefits or dangers associated with it.

When I have given workshops it is always convincing to select some strong, young man, such as a weight lifter or football player, to demonstrate the results of music upon muscular strength. I have him lift a weight which he does easily. Then he listens to rock music for only a few minutes and is asked to lift the same weight again. He is astonished to find how much his strength has diminished. That discordant beat has disrupted the body harmony and weakened him. After listening to Mozart or some harmonious composition for a short time, he finds his strength restored and he can lift the weight again without effort.

In a Maternity Hospital in Tokyo, Dr. Ikuya Oka found that the right kind of music increased the milk flow of the nursing mothers from 50% to 150%. The music used was instrumental, choir, mood or semi-classical. Swing, electronic or syncopated music caused a decrease in milk production.

An amusing incident was reported in a newspaper about a farmer who had a mother skunk establish residence for her young under the floor of his home. He tried moth balls and bait, all of the known tricks to draw her away, but nothing worked until he decided that since he couldn't stand the noise of rock music maybe the skunk couldn't either. He set his radio to a rock station and turned it up full blast. Within 24 hours the skunk had departed with her babies — and never returned.

A student in a Maryland high school did an experiment with music on mice. He played soft strains of violin music for eight hours a day and found that the mice could cut the maze-running time from 65 seconds down to 27 seconds in eight tries. The mice subjected to rock couldn't get through the maze in 300 seconds and they were found to develop confused and irritable behavior.

So much for animals. What effect do loud sounds have upon humans?

The Better Hearing Institute in Washington, D.C. has given us a table of sound decibel levels to alert us to the damage noise can bring.

Sound	Decibels	Time permitted (before damage is done)
Whispering	20 "	No limit
Average home sounds	50 "	No limit
Car (average motor)	70 "	No limit
Subway	100 "	2 hours
Rock band	115 "	*15 minutes*
Air Raid siren	130 "	3 minutes, 45 seconds.

Physical Impairment

The body adjusts to many handicaps. It can lose a lung, kidney, eyes, limbs, part of a stomach, spleen, bowel, even brain and it compensates in some manner and the person continues to function reasonably well. *But it has no defense against loud and repetitive sound.* There is no gas mask, as for air, to filter out polluted sound; no purifyer for sound, as there is for water; no reconstruction for damaged ears, as there is for damaged earth. The body is helpless against damaging sound, so it becomes the most dangerous of all pollutants; for it not only destroys the hearing, it penetrates to the marrow of one's bones. The entire body is shaken by it.

Mental Deterioration

When consciousness has to struggle to tune out interfering noise, it is put under stress as if one were trying to type or play a violin with one hand while the other was held out to ward off an enemy; or trying to walk with one leg dragging a heavy weight. It divides the attention and after a time the person becomes numbed to many things in the environment. *His alertness is severely hindered.* Not only can he no longer listen to delightful sounds such as children laughing, crickets in the evening, birds singing, wind in the trees, or beautiful music. He does not hear things which may be to his benefit such as warnings, fire sirens while he is driving, or instructions important to his job or life. His attention span is shortened. Apathy and lethargy result. To preserve itself, the mind closes in upon itself, trying to shut out the annoyances around it.

I know of people leaving a restaurant because they could not enjoy their meal in the throbbing noise imposed on them. I am not alone in having walked out of many stores before finishing shopping because the music was so irritating it was impossible to make careful selections. Waitresses in night clubs, where noise is amplified, are quickly exhausted. (The body tenses against the loud vibrations and fatigue sets in, also irritation.) Some have had to leave their jobs because they could not endure the stress. Their doctors have advised them to seek other employment.

One knowledgable musical therapist (may her tribe increase), was so annoyed by the so-called "live" music in a fashionable dining place that she complained to the management. They said, "No one else has complained so we cannot deprive other patrons of their pleasure."

Undaunted, she took a sheet of paper and went from table to table, asking the diners if they liked the music. Most said, "No, but what can we do about it?" She asked them to sign their names and took the impressive list back to the manager. He couldn't believe it at first. "Here we've been paying those musicians for annoying our guests?" At a later visit, my friend found that the pounding band had been replaced by a violin soloist.

So, we *can* do something about it. Much that is destructive and unhealthy continues because we are too timid or ignorant to correct it. This may be changed when people come to understand that NOISE IS BAD BUSINESS. It

costs in loss of customers, and causes inefficiency and
fatigue in employees.

Certain sounds carry more power than others. The "H"
or "K" sounds, such as *Hi, Hah, Hoh, Hu, Kah* and *Koo*
appear to stimulate the glandular system. It has been
explained that these particular sounds (produced by
tightening the abdominal muscles and forcing the breath
out against the roof of the mouth) cause a strong vibration
close to the pituitary area, thus causing an immediate
reaction. A Zen master told his pupils that if they would
say, "Ho! Ho!" vigorously for five minutes every day they
would never die. I don't know about that but Santa Claus
has been around for a long time. Could that be the secret
of his longevity?

If one will stand erect and repeat, in a very declarative
manner, "Hi-Ho-Hu-Ha-Hi!" the energy field will be activated and one can no more remain depressed than one
can stay on the ground floor if one steps into an express
elevator that shoots to the top.

When a room full of people do this in a joyous manner
the energy released is so strong that even recorded on a
tape, it will be contagious to a listener.* Often people will
come to a night lecture, admitting that they are very tired.
At the end of a two hour session they are so invigorated
that they feel they could go on for another session. They
realize for the first time that the increased vitality is *from
their own field.* It was there all the time but needed opportunity to be released.

Other sounds considered to have effect on the glands
and organs are listed here for you to experiment with.

---

*Toning tapes are available from Gentle Living Publications, P.O. Box 27522,
Denver, CO 80227 (see p. 84).

Ah (as in hard)	Stimulates upper lungs
Deep *O* (as in home)	Stimulates lower lungs
Ohm	Stimulates heart
OO (as in broom)	Stimulates sex glands
Ea (as in head)	Stimulates thyroid, parathyroid and throat
Ee (as in seed)	Stimulates pituitary and pineal glands, and head in general

Rahm (Toned from the solar plexus releases a sense of authority and power).

Eh-He-Ah (Toned softly is soothing and relaxing. Let it drift off in a sigh).

People have asked me questions which indicate that either I have not written very well or they have not read very well.

"Do I stand with my arms raised while I Tone?"

Not unless you wish to. The idea is, after stretching high to pull the rib cage up so that air can get into the lungs, the arms are to drop *back behind one* (not forward) so that the body is in a very erect but relaxed posture.

"How do I know if I'm doing it right?"

I ask in turn, "How does it *feel*?" Toning is feeling. *It is release.* It is a feeling of contained excitement, ready to burst out. It is the feeling of a child on Christmas morning —expectancy. If you have trouble feeling that, imagine you are a candidate for an academy award and the MC says, "The envelope, please!" (Excitement, anticipation, one-pointed attention.) "The winner is—" and your name is called! You run up to receive the award.

That is the feeling of letting the sound rise up through you, "as a siren", beginning very low, starting over and over if necessary, but each time letting it go higher until—

"the winner is—" and the sound flies up and out in sheer delight.

Then one sighs in contentment and the body, mind and soul are all together in harmony. One moves through the day feeling in full control. Acting with purpose instead of being buffeted about with reactions.

Someone may argue, "But I don't feel like Christmas morning. I don't even feel like trying to Tone."

Do it anyway. That is when you need most to Tone. It is like starting a car. Turn the key in the ignition. Start the motor. Get the engine warmed up and then decide where to go. SOUND MAKES YOU FEEL. That is the secret of its power.

While I am sure that anyone who can open the mouth and make a sound can Tone, I have come to believe very few can teach it. As I have given lectures and workshops from coast to coast, it is not unusual for people to comment before a session, "I've studied Toning with—" or, "I was taught Toning." After the session they exclaim. "This isn't what I was taught at all! This is amazing. I had no idea how powerful it could be."

It appears that most of the people who profess to be teaching it have never studied with me, attended a workshop or even heard tapes I have made. (There are four persons whom I consider qualified. Two flew in from Australia and Denmark and really studied, and two are in this country. There are several others who have a good understanding and, with several years experience, will be good teachers.)

To teach requires a great deal of study of the principles underlying the phenomena of healing, the psychological aspects and some understanding of how the brain functions. It is most necessary to develop a strong intuitive sense and experience with energy fields. Otherwise the full benefit will not be passed on to another and that one may be hindered from receiving all that might be possible if one were not trying to follow someone else's limited concept.

I have heard of some who had their students lie on the floor to Tone. Lying down may be all right for groaning. It is good for resting, sleeping, and dying, but not for Toning! (I tried it. It is impossible to get the desired results.) When the spine is horizontal it responds to magnetic currents of the earth. For spiritual or health-stimulating practice one should stand, if at all possible, or sit erect with the spine being straight so that the energy in one's field may circulate "from earth to heaven and back again."

Lightning seldom strikes a dead log. It is attracted to a tree, a rod, or something tall and upright. When one Tones, one is attracting an energy from the universal pattern which, in nature, is focused in lightning.

During a tour I saw a lecture on Toning advertised. I attended to find what was being given and perhaps learn some new aspects of it. It turned out to be the most ridiculous bellowing of gruesome sounds I had ever heard. There was no purpose or direction, nor understanding of Toning as I know it.

Toning is release of energy, but it must inspire and lift one's consciousness and be directed to constructive intention. It is not just releasing agonizing noises. From what I have gathered from studies of ancient peoples and cultures, it probably came about as primitive man responded to the beauty of a sunrise, the awe and reverence of mighty events in nature. It was an unconscious urge to lift himself, to identify with some great power of strength or beauty, or to rejoice in some victory.

With all of our intellectual achievements, we are still kin to that early man. The energy in our electro-magnetic fields must be directed to useful purpose. The energy, like water, should be channeled to fruitful distribution or it oozes away and is lost. If we do not direct our own energy, other sources will impose on it and use it for themselves. The result leaves one drained, weak and depressed, and at the mercy of whatever wishes to control.

When I first witnessed misrepresentations called "Toning," I was so dismayed that I wished I had never introduced it. But Life has a sense of humor. People insisted that they had received some help even from these misguided attempts, and I had to admit that no matter how badly they had done it, if they opened their mouths and let sound out (with expectancy) some little good would result. However, it distresses me that people who claim to be teaching Toning make charges for what, in my opinion, they are not giving.

A question often raised is, "What colors are associated with musical notes?"

There is a relationship, although sound and color are not produced in the same way. Few people will agree on which key corresponds to which color. They have received some intuitive impressions about it, which may be correct for them, but I prefer the ordered, logical sequence of notes to the prismatic pattern as given below. (This came to me through Roger Stevens, musical instructor and member of the Los Angeles Symphony, and from a book printed in the last century.)

Emotional Damage

More than any other outside factor, music governs our emotions. We can be changed from anger to tears of compassion by music. This is not through conditioning or imposed attitudes. Experiments made by Dorothy Retallack,

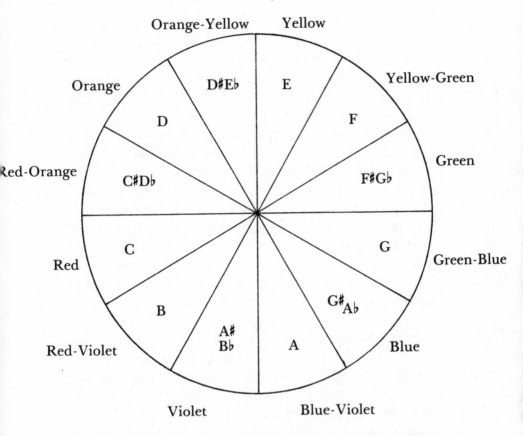

described in her book, *The Sound of Music and Plants,* *
proved how plants were killed by some music and others
flourished with different music. Surely plants do not respond because of "opinions." It was reaction of the molecular structure to the vibrations of sound.

A missionary in Africa experimented with recordings
of semi-classical music and acid-rock. He played both to
a tribe that had never heard white man's music before.
When they listened to semi-classical and harmonic music

*Sound of Music and Plants, Dorothy Retallack, DeVorss & Co., Marina del Rey,
Calif.

they responded with smiles and nods of approval and were calm and peaceful. Then, without comment, rock was played. Immediately they reacted. They became agitated. Some grabbed their spears and were ready to fight. Others threw rocks at the record player, apparently trying to kill the threatening thing.*

Rhythm controls the body and extends to whipping the mind into subjection. Mobs can be moved to violence, killing and destruction "without thinking" if drum beats and rhythms are intensified. Drums have always been used to stimulate warfare, from jungles to military marches. Early man found that drums caused the heart to quicken, excitement to grow and a group of people so unified could be directed by a single, strong command. Pagan dances and rituals are accompanied by incessant drumming. The monotonous, beating rhythms have long been used as a hypnotic tool in black magic and voodoo ceremonies.

In the entertainment world this was recognized even before the silent movie era. Stage performances were enhanced by off-stage sounds. Now background sounds (not always music) that are pounding, discordant, eerie, accompany the picture to stimulate emotions. Sounds manipulate us in TV advertising far beyond our awareness because we pay little attention to them. If they bypass our critical attention, they go directly into the subconscious and move us from there. Especially is this true in what we consider to be entertainment when we sit passively, accepting the suggestions in a hypnotic state.

The power of music over us is well portrayed in the book, *Super Learning* by Ostrander and Schroeder.

As people in the past have chosen certain medicines for

*Satan's Music Exposed, by Lowell Hart, published by Salem Kirbran, Inc., Huntington Valley, Pa.

their illness, in the future they may choose certain music for their healing. Even now people are doing that to change their moods and attitudes.

How could one remain angry if one listened to an *Ave Maria?* Or frustrated or anxious with the superb freedom suggested in *Pachelbel's Canon in D,* or Smetana's *Moldau,* or Respighi's *Fountains of Rome?* For inspiration, try Bach's *Jesu, Joy of Man's Desiring,* Berlioz' *Roman Carnival,* Grieg's *Piano Concerto,* Brahm's *Hungarian Dances,* and Handel's *Messiah.* Most of Mozart is comforting and uplifting. There are many popular songs of the romantic period in the 1950s. There is loveliness in *Lara's Song* from Dr. Zhivago, and *Send In the Clowns,* and others of a flowing, harmonious pattern.

Choose your music by melody and harmony—not the words. The music influences one's moods far more than the words. Scientific studies of the influence of rhythms on the body indicate that the waltz is most compatible with the heart beat. Syncopated jazz and rock confuse the natural body rhythm and induce stress.

"Why, then," some will ask, "are discos and rock bands so popular?"

Stress causes adrenalin to be released—the old "flight or fight" instincts are stirred. When the body is under constant stress it may become addicted to the adrenalin flow, as with any drug, and feels the need of it. Many people are "hooked" on this sense of agitation and become adrenalin junkies. They think that they cannot work or study without that stimulation, but the tension in the body (and drain on the pancreas) takes its toll. It weakens or destroys the body as any addiction destroys through enslavement.

When we are selective of the influences we permit to

come into our environments, we are more able to with-stand the destructive elements—sounds of industry, travel, etc.—over which we have no control. We use our voices, and the sounds we select, as a kind of sound barrier of protection around us and we are able to keep our peace and stability in that quiet center within, in spite of outside storms.

The voice belongs to the body and is its instrument. We, being more than the body, should use it as a tool for higher consciousness. Rather than being a battle-ground between freedom of spirit and enslavement to sense-indulgence, it should be a vehicle for refinement. (The Dalai Lama said, during a visit to this country, "Anger, expressed, only multiplies and increases.") Instead of per-mitting the voice to express anger, hatred, fear, self-pity and greed in loud, ugly language, we should direct it to transform our lives into their rightful potential.

Sir Edwin Arnold expressed it so beautifully in *The Light of Asia:*

> *Right Discourse:* Govern the lips
> As they were palace-doors, the King within;
> Tranquil and fair and courteous be all words
> Which from that presence win.

The person using his voice in that manner creates a beautiful and harmonious life. It is not meekness nor weakness, but quiet control. Speaking is an expression of will. Will is the divine authority to choose. Choice is the framework or structure of our lives. The choices we have made result in what we are and have today. What we choose today creates the pattern for our future.

The ability to speak is a holy gift. We should use it

with responsibility and reverence. We should be fully aware that this great energy of Life is ours to direct. In Toning we meet it where it is, in its pristine, childlike state; we refine it, lovingly direct it to its greatest usefulness, and offer it up as a communion cup we have fashioned, to receive the essence of Life's best gifts; and then, to offer it to others.

BIBLIOGRAPHY

Andrews, Donald Hatch. *The Symphony of Life*, Lee's Summit, Mo., Unity Books, 1966

Assagioli, Roberto. *Psychosynthesis*, N. Y., Viking Press, 1965

Bach, Marcus. *The Inner Ecstasy*, Nashville, Tenn., Abingdon Press, 1969

Barnett, Lincoln. *The Universe & Dr. Einstein*, New York, Harper Bros., 1948

Day & DeLaWarr. *Matter in the Making*, London, Vincent Stuart, 1970

DeBit, Ralph M. *Healing Technic* and *Clear Thinking*, Denver, Colo., Cooper Press, 1946

DeBit, Ralph M. *Problem of Good & Evil*, Santa Barbara, Ca., Rowny Press, 1959

Flanagan, G. Patrick. *The Pyramid and Its Relationship to Biocosmic Energy*, Glendale, Ca., 1972

Green, Elmer. *Biofeedback for Mind-Body Self-Regulation; Healing & Creativity*, Los Altos, Ca., Academy of Parasychology & Medicine, 1971

Hall, Manly P. *Secret Teachings of All Ages*, Los Angeles, Ca., Philosophical Research Society, Inc., 1928

Heisenberg, Werner. *Physics & Beyond*, New York, Harper & Row, 1971

Higgins, Godfrey. *Anacalypsis*, New Hyde Park, N. Y. University Books, 1963

Hills, Christopher. *Nuclear Evolution*, London. Centre Com. Pub., 1968

Jacobi, Jolande. *Psychology of Carl Jung*, New Haven, Conn. Yale University Press, 1951

Kilner, Walter J. *The Human Aura,* New Hyde Park, N. Y., University Books, 1965

Kingsland, William. *The Gnosis of Ancient Wisdom in Christian Scriptures,* Wheaton, Ill., Theosophical Pub., 1937

Kuhn, Alvin B. *Lost Key to the Scriptures & Shadow of Third Century,* Wheaton, Ill., Theosophical Pub., 1972

Murchie, Guy. *Music of the Spheres,* N. Y., Dover Pub., 1967

Ostrander & Schroeder, *Psychic Discoveries Behind the Iron Curtain,* Englewood Cliffs, N. J., Prentice-Hall, 1970

Ouspensky, P. K. *The Fourth Way,* N. Y., Vintage Books, 1957

Pike, Albert. *Morals & Dogma,* Richmond, Va., Jenkins Pub., 1914

Tiller, William. *Radionics, Radiesthesia & Physics,* Los Altos, Ca., Academy of Parapsychology & Medicine, 1971

Tompkins, Peter. *Secrets of the Great Pyramid,* N. Y., Harper & Row, 1971

Waters, Frank. *The Book of the Hopi,* N. Y., Viking Books, 1963